To Wendy and Paul

Lessons Learned
A Practicioner's Guide to Successful Marketing

With best wishes

AA

Alvin Achenbaum

© 2014 Achenbaum Institute of Marketing

ISBN : 978-0-9909230-0-8 (print)

For Stanley

Foreward	*i*
Why I Wrote this Book	*1*
Introduction	*5*

Lesson 1:

Building and protecting a strong brand identity is key to success in any business

The History of Branding	*12*
The introduction of trademarks	*14*
The Concept of Brand Value	*15*
Author's Contribution: The Basic Brand Asset Model	*18*
Product, Marketing and Brand Equities	*19*
A fourth asset: management equity	*20*
Case Study: *The Nestlé Company*	*24*

Lesson 2:

Understanding consumer attitudes and behavior is fundamental to designing a meaningful brand strategy

Market Segmentation	*34*
Author's Contribution: The integration of psychological perceptions with quantitative analysis to identify consumers and define market segments	*41*
Case Study: *The Block Drug Company*	*43*
Case Study: *A Brand Positioning Statement*	*46*
Case Study: *Hanes Hosiery*	*50*
Case Study: *Clairol Hair Care*	*51*

Lesson 3:

Keeping up with an ever-changing marketplace requires disciplined strategic marketing planning

Author's Contribution: *The development of a systematic strategic marketing planning process*	56
Case Study: A Sample Marketing Plan	64
Case Study: Failure to Execute a Plan	65

Lesson 4:

The application of science to marketing makes brand management more professional and improves results

Market Research: An Overview	75
Case Study: Jif Peanut Butter	87
Case Study: New Coke	89
Market Testing: An Overview	91
Author's Contribution: *The creation of a novel, systematic approach to testing market variables*	96
Case Study: The H&R Block Company	96

Lesson 5:

Identifying real media exposure is critical to evaluating advertising effectiveness

The Role of Advertising	*108*
Guidelines for Successful Brand Communications	*110*
Author's Contribution: *The development of the effective rating point tool to improve the assessment of advertising effectiveness*	*115*
The Effective Exposure Theory	*116*

Lesson 6:

A successful client-agency partnership will drive business and brand performance

Guidelines for Effective Client-Agency Partnerships	*123*
Author's Contribution: *The creation of a system for identifying the right communications agency partner*	*129*
Case Study: Toyota Motors	*137*
Author's Contribution: *The development of a tailored agency compensation agreement to ensure results*	*139*
Guidelines for an Equitable Client-Agency Partnership	*140*
Case Study: A Sample Compensation Agreement	*146*

Conclusion	*151*
Acknowledgements	*157*
About the Author	*159*

j

Foreword

By Jon Achenbaum

While my personal view is naturally biased, I hope that you will permit me to share with you why I believe that Alvin Achenbaum, my father, is the best person to provide you with a primer on marketing. While he had superb academic training, it is Al's experience in the business trenches, as a researcher, an innovator and an advisor with a taste for controversy, which best qualifies him to provide applicable Lessons on how marketing should be practiced. As you will see, many of Al's ideas challenged and changed the way marketers, advertisers and even practitioners like you work today. I believe that there is much to be learned from his Lessons.

Al's career took off just as the "Mad Men" era was getting underway and it was his good fortune to observe and participate in many fundamental changes in the marketing and advertising worlds. In fact, it is Al's many decades of working, first as a market researcher, then as a marketing planner and strategist, and eventually as a senior executive and consultant – which provided him with an unprecedented breadth of empirical learning – and which best qualify him to be your guide.

In all, Al spent more than 60 years as a practitioner, 20 at four different agencies and 40 as a marketing consultant to both agencies and companies across the globe. He wrote hundreds of research studies, presentations, articles and speeches, some of which changed the nature of best practices across many industries. Although he first started giving speeches in the early 1960s, the fundamentals he spoke about throughout the years have not changed much. In fact, we seem to be discussing many of the same issues today.

As it often goes with innovators, the ideas which Al proposed were not always met with universal support. He has always loved a good argument and was proud when, in the 1970s, his controversial ideas on issues like negotiating agency compensation and evaluating media effectiveness earned him the moniker "the most hated man on Madison Avenue." As you will see, however, eventually, many of his so-called blasphemous theories became integral to modern marketing practices.

This book includes a comprehensive review of the key marketing and advertising innovations which, as a practitioner, Al helped create and which are still practiced today. These include:

- Building a basic brand asset model
- Designing a consumer-driven, meaningful brand strategy
- Creating a disciplined strategic marketing planning process
- Conducting scientifically-based, quantitative market segmentation analysis
- Evaluating advertising based on effective media exposure
- Launching a systematic competitive agency search process
- Developing equitable, tailored agency compensation agreements

These ideas shook up the business environment in which they were developed, ultimately having a profound impact on the way many of today's leading global companies operate.

A Practitioner's Perspective

Over the years, Al was fortunate to have the privilege of working with and advising companies which were major players in a wide range of product and service categories. The following list highlights some of them and gives you an idea of the scope of his experience.

- Major packaged food and beverage companies, such as *Kraft Foods, Nestlé, Procter & Gamble, Coca-Cola, Seagram's* and the *Miller Brewing Company*
- Major appliance and electronics companies, such as *General Electric, Phillips, Minolta* and *RCA*
- Motor vehicle manufacturers, including *Toyota, Honda, Nissan, General Motors, Ford* and *Chrysler*
- Telecommunications giants, such as *IBM, GTE, AT&T* and *Verizon*
- Fast food restaurants, including *Wendy's, McDonald's* and *Dunkin' Donuts*
- Leading players in other fields, including *Exxon, Hallmark, Macy's,* and *NBC*

It is important to note that Al's accomplishments reflect a decided bias toward science. Much of his early work grew directly out of his belief that, as it had in the development of the medical, engineering and legal fields, incorporating scientific principles could revolutionize business practices. However, unlike most academics, who base their theories solely on untested insights and assumptions, Al always looked to find an empirical theory based on an observed reality.

In practice, by applying well-crafted quantitative market research methods to business problems, Al was able to achieve sound and actionable results. Importantly, these findings often reinforced, but occasionally refuted, the intuition and judgment of those closest to a particular project. With decades of refinement and analysis, the scientific processes Al developed have proven essential to addressing a multitude of business questions – from tweaking the packaging on a minor brand being repositioned – to making wholesale changes to the management structure of a large, complex corporation.

I hope that, as I always have, you find meaning in Dad's valuable Lessons.

Jon Achenbaum
President and CEO, Newhall Laboratories
Stamford, Connecticut
May 2014

Why I Wrote this Book

by Alvin Achenbaum

I wrote this book in part because I believe very strongly that there is a need in business today to re-establish the critical role marketing plays in economic success. Marketing is a crucial component of the free competitive market system, which has its roots in earliest civilization, and is being vastly underutilized today.

Beginning at the end of World War II and continuing until the early 1970s, marketing enjoyed a Golden Age in the United States. During that time, it played an integral role in the country's economic prosperity – what one of America's most distinguished economists, John Kenneth Galbraith, called the "Affluent Society."

But America's marketing pre-eminence no longer exists. In the past few decades, marketing has been eclipsed by changes in corporate priorities and the financial structure of the business economy. It has been whittled down by a series of self-inflicted, counterproductive responses by corporate management to the maturation of key sectors of America's dynamic economy.

I believe that companies today need to be re-educated about the central role that marketing plays in economic activity. A new generation of innovative managers needs to understand how critical marketing is to retaining brand leadership and to ensuring long-term financial health. Beginning right now, U.S. businesses must dramatically improve their use of marketing effectiveness – and they must help the rest of the world to do the same.

The Critical Role of Marketing

My goal for this book is to use my experience as a marketing practitioner to provide practical, experience-based Lessons which illuminate the critical role which marketing plays in all business success.

More specifically, I will do the following:

- Provide a comprehensive review of how marketing and brand development are critical to a company's efforts to achieve a competitive advantage and long-term financial success.
- Offer a historical and contemporary framework for the main institutions of marketing, especially market research, advertising and media planning.
- Share real-life stories of brand successes and failures to provide insight into how marketing and research influenced those outcomes.
- Enumerate the critical role that marketing planning and preparedness will play in the increasingly global and technologically complex business world of the future.

It is my hope that the ideas presented here will inspire a conversation about getting the practice of marketing back on track.

I truly believe that, no matter what field of business you are in – whether you work for a manufacturer, a retailer, an advertising agency or an online publishing firm – you can benefit from the Lessons in this book. Whether you are a planner, an overseer or an implementer, you are a practitioner of marketing, and you help make the cash register ring.

In the end, I hope that my readers will apply the Lessons in this book not only to improving the success of their businesses and to ensuring the the longevity of their careers, but also to becoming more savvy consumers every day.

Alvin Achenbaum
New York, New York
May 2014

Introduction

The business world today is very different from the one I entered in 1951, when I took my first position in the research department at the *McCann-Erickson Advertising Agency*. Market research was a relatively new, unproven field. A handful of major corporations produced and distributed a majority of the country's national brands. Television advertising was just emerging as a promising communications vehicle, and three major networks controlled almost all the viewing. Management relied on crude research tools to make critical sales and investment decisions. Most importantly, marketing was a newcomer, the first primers were yet to be published – and it constituted a vast opportunity.

Who could have imagined that, six decades later, global corporations would manage large, diversified portfolios, often with competing brands, and featuring multiple offerings under each label? That inventive technology would lead to an information explosion, where highly-tuned market research techniques could pinpoint the most targeted needs of consumers? That television viewing would be facilitated by an ever-evolving electronics industry, and that program choice, and therefore advertising access, could be controlled by the viewer? Further, who could have predicted the emergence of a highly competitive global business environment where management would emphasize short-term profits at the expense of long-term brand-building investment?

Finally, and most significantly for our purposes, who could have predicted that there would still remain an opportunity to develop uniquely positioned brands which could effectively compete in an increasingly complex and unpredictable marketplace?

I hope to convince you in this book that, despite these monumental changes, business success can still be attained via true brand leadership. All that's required is an adherence to systematic, quantifiably-based research, in concert with disciplined hard-nosed planning, and accompanied by the judicious use of all available resources – strategic, analytical, financial and human. I believe that my six decades as a practitioner qualify me to guide you in understanding how this process can really work.

Six Fundamental Lessons

The Lessons I offer in this book answer several fundamental questions which every good marketer should ask. These questions, most of which can be addressed by the application of systems which I helped develop over the years, will lead to the creation of a brand with a meaningful identity and which is well positioned to achieve positive results in the marketplace.

Here then is a preview of my Lessons and the questions they are intended to answer. Within each Lesson, I will share my unique contributions to the process, developed and refined during my years as a practitioner in the field.

Lesson 1 addresses the fundamental questions: What is my product? Does its brand name describe it effectively? What are the unique properties which distinguish it from its competition? In this Lesson, we will outline a systematic process for building a strong brand identity. We will see that, by rigorously applying the ***Basic Brand Asset Model,*** a marketer can create a meaningful brand proposition uniquely poised to compete in a complex marketplace.

Lesson 2 guides a marketer in identifying the ideal consumer for a brand. It asks: Who is my market target? What's the positioning or buying incentive for my brand? Who am I most likely to convince to purchase my product? In this Lesson, I will explain how a comprehensive consumer survey methodology, called the ***Market Target/Buying Incentive Study***, can provide valuable insight into the realities of consumer attitudes and behavior. By integrating psychological perceptions with quantitative analysis, this powerful research tool will help identify the ideal consumer for a product.

The questions raised in **Lesson 3** relate to translating a brand's strategy into an effective action plan. This Lesson asks: How do I market my brand to maximize its potential? What are my goals, in terms of volume, share and profit? What specific strategies and tactics will best help me achieve success in the marketplace? Undertaking the disciplined ***Strategic Marketing Planning Process*** which I developed will be key to achieving these goals.

Lesson 4 addresses the critical role that the application of science plays in brand success. It answers the questions: Which quantifiably-based research methods will provide actionable and replicable results? And, once a plan in place, how do I evaluate the effectiveness of its variables or core elements? My contribution to this effort was the creation of a novel, systematic approach to testing marketing variables called the ***Checkerboard Test***. This research method accurately projects marketplace results and therefore guides both strategic plan development and implementation.

Lesson 5 focuses very specifically on the effectiveness of a brand's communications strategy. The questions it addresses are: How can I determine if my advertising is reaching the appropriate consumers and, just as important, is it reaching them with enough frequency to convince them to purchase my product? The concept of assessing advertising effectiveness using the scientifically-based *Effective Rating Point Tool* remains the standard by which many media plans are judged today.

Finally, **Lesson 6** addresses some different questions, also related to ensuring great brand communications. They are: Which agency partner will best help me achieve my strategic goals? And how do I ensure that my communications budget is being well spent? My groundbreaking initiatives for building successful client-agency partnerships took the guesswork out of answering these questions. My two specific contributions were: 1) the creation of a systematic *Competitive Agency Search Process* guaranteed to match client needs with agency skills, and 2) the development of an equitable *Tailored Agency Compensation Agreement*. If applied in combination, these processes will lead to the creation of a mutually-beneficial working relationship, as well as long-term business success.

Before we begin, I must proffer one editorial consideration. This book is about brands which exist in many forms. Brands are products, such as packaged goods, automobiles or health and beauty aids. They are also services, such as personal banking, life insurance or tax preparation. A store is a brand – whether it's online or down the block. However, for simplicity's sake, throughout this text, I will be using the term "product" to refer to all types of brands.

Experience in the Marketplace

In the course of my 60-year career, I worked at four communications agencies and managed three consulting firms. I advised and aided over 150 clients, from Fortune 500 powerhouses to novice single-brand start-ups. I saw first-hand the challenges that marketers faced, what worked and didn't work in the marketplace, as well as the opportunities offered by approaching marketing challenges using systematic planning and empirical research methods. Through these experiences, and with the co-operation of some intrepid clients eager to answer core strategic questions, I was able to make important contributions to general marketing practices today.

So, journey with me now as I share the valuable Lessons which I learned as a veteran practitioner, working with my clients to test hypotheses and to address consumers' ever-changing needs. You will surely see how it is the determined application of great marketing which is the key to good management decision-making and, ultimately, to success in today's complicated and competitive business world.

Lesson 1:

Building and protecting a strong brand identity is key to success in any business

"Factories rust away, packages become obsolete, products lose their relevance. But great brands live forever – if you nurture them."

*– George Patterson,
Pioneering Advertising Executive*

Any discussion of marketing must by necessity begin with the subject of brands. In this Lesson, I will introduce many of the important concepts which will guide us throughout this text. While some of the material may seem a bit academic, I believe it will reveal that, for brands to have success in the marketplace, their managers must judiciously apply a rigorous, scientifically-based process to every phase of a brand's development. We will begin with the evolution of the first trademarked brands, then introduce the concept of brand value, outlining the four key qualities – or equities – which are essential to the distinction of a brand from its competition. Next we will identify the **Basic Brand Asset Model**, which has become the generally accepted practice in the development of brands today. Finally, I will share what I believe are the critical components of successful brand management. As you will see, these depend on a commitment to building and supporting brand equity – from the management at the top of the organization all the way down to the retail shelf.

The History of Branding

Brands – or trademarks – are integral to the world we live in today. Your car, your shirt, your beverage, even the lettuce on your salad – each of these has a brand name (and a company) associated with it. And while you probably aren't conscious of it, your choice of a particular product is the result of determined behind-the-scenes efforts by a dedicated team of marketers working to ensure that you are aware of a brand, appreciate its unique characteristics and, most importantly, will choose it over the competition.

In order to appreciate the value of great brands, it's important to understand their history. While brands as we know them came into existence in the early 1900s, their value was only truly appreciated and maximized over the last half century. Today brands are what make a successful company thrive. A brief review of the evolution of brands – from commodities to sophisticated icons – is an excellent place to begin our discussion of why building and protecting a brand's identity is the most important thing a marketer can do.

Until the Industrial Revolution and the emergence of the factory system, there was very little competition among sellers and buyers. Once the steam engine was invented in 1775, trade grew exponentially, as factories in Great Britain and later in the United States churned out products that had to be traded in order for their manufacturers to remain solvent. Products were sold relatively freely, with sellers competing with other sellers and buyers with other buyers.

The first competition was essentially for commodities, or raw materials – food from the farms, fish from the sea, metal ores, oil, cotton and wood. Commodities, by definition, are not associated with a specific seller because they carry no trademark. Most are standardized items that are sometimes graded in terms of quality or size. Typically, they are known by a generic descriptor – for example, apples – but additional descriptors are often used to further differentiate them, such as Granny Smith or Roma.

Many foodstuffs that at one time were considered commodities are now sold under brand names. An example is *Sunkist* oranges, which are grown by a cooperative of California farmers. *Ocean Spray* gave a brand name to cranberries, as did *Perdue* to chicken. Unlike a quarter century ago, today commodities like bananas, pineapples, tomatoes and mushrooms all sport brand names, as do eggs and milk.

So far, the branded products we have been discussing are all food products. However, you will see that our discussion of brands will be a comprehensive one, including branded products in categories like health and beauty aids, automobiles, financial services and even retail stores. So, it's important for me to establish upfront that, while I will use the term "product" to refer to brands throughout this text, for simplicity's sake, "product" refers to all types of brands and services.

The introduction of trademarks

The most critical factor influencing the development of branded products came about when the U.S. Government, beginning in 1870, enacted laws concerning trademarks, which specified how sellers and buyers could identify and view products competitively as brands.

It is important to note that trademarks and brands existed long before trademark laws were enacted. They started to emerge as soon as people and governments realized the value of identifying commercial purveyors. The word brand comes from the imprinting of a name or symbol – on a package, on metal or on an animal – to designate its owner. The branding of cattle, barrels and silver flatware goes back a very long time.

Technically, a brand is a registered trademark which is owned by the registrant. The owner has exclusive use of the trademark as long as he or she continues to use it. By law, no one else can encroach on its use in any way. Any seller has the right to obtain a registered trademark as long as no one else already has it.

The government began to recognize and register trademarks in 1870, when the Commission of Patents was established. This office had the jurisdiction to make appropriate rules and regulations concerning trademarks. The first exclusive trademark was enacted in 1905 and, by 1946, about a half a million trademarks had been registered.

The Concept of Brand Value

Now that we've defined what a branded or trademarked product is, we can examine why it is so important to both manufacturers and consumers. Not only is a brand a name, but it also has a unique value, which clearly distinguishes it from a commodity. In essence, **Brand Value** is the sum total of a consumer's perceptions, emotions and feelings about a product's attributes, its marketing activities, the brand name itself and the reputation of the company associated with it. **Brand Value** is what gives a brand its equity and, if carefully cultivated and nurtured, gives a seller leverage, often allowing a seller to put a premium price on a product.

Just trademarking a product does not necessarily dictate its success, however. Choosing the best trademark – or brand name – can have a major influence on its value in the marketplace. Here are some key questions a seller should ask when developing a brand name:

1) Is the brand name associated with an established company product, service or institution, and is what it stands for appropriate?

2) Does the brand's reputation adequately differentiate it from its competitors and give it an advantage in its marketing?

3) Do the logo and product descriptor identify it effectively and help communicate what it stands for?

If a marketer follows these guidelines, assuming that the product is a strong proposition in itself, it is much more likely to see success in the marketplace.

But we are getting a bit ahead of our story. Originally, most companies made a single product and were single brand companies, e.g., *The Quaker Oats Company* which, of course, harvested and sold rolled oats. Over time, companies began to diversify, in some cases entering additional product categories – in other cases offering variously priced products, and in still others cases competing in more than one brand category. This process became even more complicated at the end of the 20th century as, in order to grow, companies bought other companies which had products in new categories and with new brands. Until then, companies almost always gave a new brand name to any new product in a given category. Soon after, companies began expanding globally, introducing similar products under different brand names in different countries. Clearly, choosing a trademark and launching a brand in the marketplace had become a complicated business. Thus, understanding the value of a brand versus its competition became a critical factor for success in the marketplace.

One of the first studies that our consulting firm undertook was an analysis of the value of brands. It was in the 1970s, when companies were rapidly expanding, moving from a single brand entity to a diverse portfolio of brands. Our clients were anxious to better understand what the value of a brand was and how to put it to its maximum use. Thus, our firm identified a series of **Brand Values** to help guide marketers eager give their brands the best competitive advantage. In all, we identified nine **Brand Values** – five for the seller and four for the buyer.

The seller's perspective

A brand offers five key values or advantages to its seller.

The first type of brand value for the seller is ***recognition value***. Branding simplifies marketing communications, especially advertising, by enabling the buyer to readily recognize and identify the seller of the product. This is the role which the trademark plays.

The second type of brand value is *availability value*. Branding allows the seller to tell prospective buyers via advertising and promotion where it is available, that is, in which distribution channels the brand can be found.

The third brand value is *confidence value*. Through branding, the seller conveys to the buyer that its product is of uniform quality whenever and wherever it is bought.

The fourth brand value is *image value*. Branding can convey information and perceptions about a product and its various qualities – what it contains, how it is made, how it is to be used, what it stands for, its price, the seller's or owner's reputation, as well as the possible benefits it can provide for the purchaser. Because claims about a product can be attributed to its brand name, the brand's owner is held responsible for any representations made about it.

The final advantage for the seller is *defensive value*. Branding prevents other marketers or sellers from being directly identified with the branded item because the brand legally belongs to its seller. In this sense, every brand in the same product category is different and therefore protected.

The buyer's perspective

While brands offer sellers much value, they offer buyers a great deal as well.

First, brands offer *recourse value*. A buyer who is dissatisfied with the purchase knows he can return a branded item to its manufacturer. The brand name tells buyers who is responsible for redressing any problem with the item.

Second, brands offer consumers assurance of *uniform quality.* The quality and form of the branded item will not vary no matter whenever and wherever it is purchased.

Third, brands offer *ease of identity.* Buyers can readily recognize their preferred brand because other sellers are not permitted to copy a product's logo, name or packaging.

Fourth, brands offer *information value.* Companies make it easy for consumers to acquire information about a brand, for example, on the package, through advertising, or on a website.

So you can see that, from a corporate standpoint, it makes sense for a manufacturer to brand its products. Its value derives from the particular brand's familiarity and its reputation with respect to the competition. The product's value further helps a brand gain and retain consumer brand loyalty, and allows the company to charge a premium price for it.

Author's Contribution: The development and implementation of the Basic Brand Asset Model

While the value of brands to both buyers and sellers is obvious to most manufacturers today, in the early 1970s, there was a great deal of disagreement over how to ensure that a brand's value was being maximized. At that time, my consulting firm was asked to develop a conceptual model for assessing the value of a brand, as well as its competitive position. We named this the ***Basic Brand Asset Model.*** Counter to conventional wisdom at the time, we asserted that brands comprise not one, but three types of equities, which together make up its ***Brand Asset Value.*** We began by asking three important questions:

1) Does the seller deliver a product of better value than its competitors?

2) Has the seller marketed its brands better than the competition?

3) Do consumers know about the seller's brands and think they are better than the competition?

By carefully answering these questions, it is possible for a marketer to determine how a specific brand stacks up against its competition. The ultimate aim of this analysis, of course, is to determine how a brand's market position can be sustained or possibly improved. Our research identified a systematic method for approaching this challenge: by evaluating the business on three separate dimensions: product, marketing and brand equities.

Product, Marketing and Brand Equities

Here then are the specific features of the three types of equities which comprise a brand's asset value:

Product Equity is a measure of the product's value versus its competitors. It represents the objective quality and performance of the product or service itself, its assortment and uniformity, its nomenclature, its price, its warranties and guarantees and, when relevant, its packaging. The relationship of all of these attributes to a brand's price represents its price-value ratio and suggests how much of a premium price it can demand.

Marketing Equity addresses how well the product is marketed versus its competition. It encompasses product distribution, pricing, personal selling and sales aids, merchandising and promotional activities, product publicity, direct marketing, as well as advertising to consumers and, when relevant, to the trade.

Brand Equity measures what consumers know and think about a brand versus its competition. It is the result achieved by evaluating the way *Product Equity* and *Marketing Equity* are used together to assess the buyers' familiarity with the brand name and their perception of the brand's attributes. In other words, it measures consumers' perceptions of the brand's reputation and predicts their propensity to buy that brand and remain loyal to it. In Lesson 2, we will examine how using quantitative analysis to underscore consumer behavior will further lead to the development of a meaningful brand strategy.

Once our firm defined brand assets in terms of these three equities – *Product, Marketing and Brand Equities* – it was then possible to use quantitative measures to determine a brand's value in the marketplace relative to its competition. Marketers can assess a brand's performance on various criteria – such as increased unit volume, increased revenue generation, increased market share, and increased profit. Although this type of analysis is somewhat subjective, knowledgeable people in the industry understand how an assessment like this can articulate which competitive brands stand out, and why.

While the value of determining these three equities for a product is obvious, it was the discovery of a fourth brand asset – *Management Equity* – which truly completed the picture.

A fourth asset: management equity

The *Basic Brand Asset Model* our firm developed became a mainstay of many corporations' early marketing efforts. A few years after we completed the model, the management at *Dunkin' Donuts* came to us and asked us to more thoroughly examine the factors that contribute to the long-term maintenance of a successful, dominant brand. To ascertain this, we conducted a content analysis of the business literature for ten iconic brands, as well as for three brands which had failed in the marketplace. In the process, we discovered that there is an additional asset for our model which we had not recognized at first: a company's leadership or its **Management Equity**.

Management Equity answers a critical fourth question: Does the company leader have a vision of what he/she wants to provide to consumers?

Our research showed that a company's top management plays an integral role in creating and sustaining an iconic brand. A CEO must have a meaningful vision for a brand which truly resonates with consumers and distinguishes the product from its competition. If he or she consistently implements this vision throughout the organization, there is substantial assurance of business success.

Thus, our firm modified our **Basic Brand Asset Model** to incorporate **Management Equity**. I am proud to say that researchers and marketers today still use this four-tiered method to determine why and how a brand stacks up versus its competitors.

The Brand Name

Now that we understand the four most important factors, or Equities, for evaluating a brand's success, let's turn to a discussion of how a brand name is interpreted by the consumer. History has shown that successful brands have a clear function articulated by their product descriptor. However, if the brand is carefully nurtured, its brand name will mean much more than that to the consumer.

Product descriptors are the words that describe a product category – and are tied to branding. For *Kleenex,* the product descriptor is facial tissue. For *Gillette,* it's blades and razors. For a brand name to work, it must have a clear-cut generic descriptor describing what it is, for example, powdered soap, condensed soup or sub-compact automobile. The generic descriptor has a value in itself. It allows a seller to tell the buyer clearly and precisely what type of product or service it sells.

A brand name is not the same as a product descriptor. If consumers begin to think of a brand that way, the brand is vulnerable to being "delisted," that is, the government can revoke the company's right to use the brand name exclusively. For example, aspirin was delisted by the government because its original manufacturer, *Bayer*, failed to call the product by its brand name plus its product descriptor: Aspirin Brand, an analgesic. Two companies we conducted research for, *Kleenex* and *Formica*, came close to losing their trademarks for similar reasons when nearly everyone called all facial tissues Kleenex and all laminated boards Formica. Fortunately, through judicious communications efforts, these companies were able to protect their trademarks.

One of our early research studies showed that, in order to ensure that a brand has value beyond its product descriptor, several differentiating factors must be in place:

- It must resonate with a sizeable market
- It must be priced to be perceived as having value
- It must be service-oriented to satisfy the consumer in every way
- It must be consistent in the service it offers, that is, a reliable brand
- It must have a production and distribution infrastructure in place so that it is poised to grow quickly
- It must have an advertising and publicity campaign effective in generating awareness and promoting its image

These factors, in conjunction with a consistent effort to communicate a brand's specific trademark, are key to ensuring that a brand will never be considered simply a product descriptor.

Brand Architecture

In 1999, the Nestlé Company asked our firm to help address a different branding issue, **Brand Architecture.** The concept of **Brand Architecture** is particularly relevant in the business world today, where corporations have large portfolios of brands which cross many categories.

Many individual brands have been around for years. For example, *Levi's Blue Jeans* and *Maxwell House Coffee* were registered as trademarks in 1873, *Budweiser Beer* in 1876, *Ivory Soap* in 1879, *Coca-Cola* in 1886 and *Campbell's Soup* in 1898. By and large, brand names initially were attached to packaged food and beverages. Larger scale machinery followed closely, with manufacturers trademarking names like *Ford*, *General Electric* and *Singer*. Later, designer names became brands, such as *Calvin Klein* and *Coach*.

As we identified earlier, the first companies to trademark their products offered a single brand which could be easily associated with its manufacturer. In the 1980s, companies began to diversify, entering additional product categories, offering differently priced brands, and ultimately acquiring companies in entirely new categories or even countries. This multiplicity of brands led to the need to rationalize the use of various brand names within one corporation. Thus emerged the concept of **Brand Architecture.**

Case Study: The Nestlé Company

When the *Nestlé Company's* executives approached us, they were concerned that they there was too much overlap and confusion about their vast array of brands and subsidiaries. We proposed a rationalization of the company's roster into a hierarchical structure, which would help dictate both its internal marketing organization and its external communications strategies.

After reviewing *Nestlé's* myriad businesses, we created an easily applied **Brand Architecture**. We identified four levels of brands within the corporation. This structure logically delineated the Nestlé products. Here is that **Brand Architecture**, illustrated by brands which are still reflected in the *Nestlé* portfolio today.

Corporate brand: A stand-alone company that acts as the umbrella for all other brands associated with it. (*The Nestlé Company*)

Company brand: Products of a stand-alone company that the buying public doesn't associate with a corporate brand. (*Nestlé's Carnation Company*, which includes Evaporated Milk and Coffeemate)

Range brand: A brand that is largely an umbrella subsidiary with other brand names under it. (*Nestlé Confections*, which includes a range of regional and national brands, such as Nestlé Crunch, Baby Ruth, Gobstoppers and Abuelita)

Product-specific brand: A brand not associated with a superior brand name in the hierarchy and not a sub-brand for a specific product type of a range brand. (Poland Spring, Perrier and San Pellegrino, all part of *Nestlé Waters*)

You may have been surprised to learn that those three major brands of bottled water, which clearly compete against each other yet have unique consumer positions, are part of the same company. That is an excellent testament to the brand management system.

Guidelines for a Successful Brand Management System

Now that we've established how a brand can be best integrated into a corporate structure, it is time to examine one of the most critical factors in ensuring its long-term success: the quality of stewardship. The **Brand Management System,** which was created in the 1930s by the *Procter & Gamble Company,* underwent many iterations on its path to becoming the dominant organizational structure for virtually every company which manages brands today. This system proved revolutionary in helping companies to distinguish their brands from the competition and to effectively addressing changes in the marketplace. It has been equally important in helping marketers ensure that, no matter how large or small, every brand's value is maximized.

A **Brand Management System** is only as good as the organizational structure and corporate leadership which support it. In my experience, there are several guidelines to ensuring the successful management of a brand.

Install a CEO with vision

As noted above, in our seminal research for *Dunkin' Donuts,* we learned that business success depends largely on having a CEO with a specific vision and a commitment to building brand equity above all else. In particular, the CEO must be:

- Dedicated, focused and meticulous in implementing the vision
- Adaptable to external changes in the marketplace consistent with this vision
- Respectful of research and innovative in extending a brand's success
- A motivating leader who recognizes true achievements among employees and within brands

Implement a solid brand management structure

The *Brand Management System* is designed to give each brand an internal advocate who can harness the power of a company's vast support system – advertising and promotions agencies, sales force, R&D, supply chain, etc. However, it is critical that managers be given the authority and responsibility to direct the brand's marketing team. Company leaders must:

- Create an umbrella marketing management structure to oversee all of the brands in a single product category
- Give marketing managers responsibility for integrating the entire marketing communications mix
- Include a trade-marketing function in the marketing structure

Have a long-term orientation

In today's economy, Wall Street's hunger for short-term profits makes long-term branding decisions difficult for all but the strongest, most financially independent companies. As a result, companies experience greater management turnover, engage in outsourcing and do not engender loyalty among employees. All of these activities create the potential for brands to lose equity, and marketers must be vigilant in trying to prevent this. To ensure brand equity is sustained, corporate leaders must:

- Seek a basis for more effectively dealing with Wall Street's demands for short-term earnings
- Agree on the desirability of brand optimization over an extended timeframe and don't permit more short-sighted profit-maximization strategies
- Ensure that sales and profit targets have been translated down to the lowest level in the marketing hierarchy

Use research to maintain brand equity

It is ironic to me that in today's marketplace of limited growth, short-term financial orientation and minimal resource allocation, marketers do not engage in more meaningful and actionable research. A great deal of research today lacks validity. Its methods are antiquated and its interpretation and implementation are often random and misguided. Many research methods, especially qualitative, fail to gain insights from consumers, who are increasingly educated, sophisticated, indifferent and even alienated. If everything we have been saying about building and sustaining brand equity is true, market research should be designed to gain maximum input from the consumer. Further, its interpretation should clearly dictate meaningful action steps. Thus, in order to ensure that a brand's quality is maximized and it is distinguished from its competitors, marketers should:

- Conduct ongoing satisfaction studies to better understand the interests and needs of both their consumers and customers
- Use quantitative consumer research to test product changes, especially to inferior elements
- Carefully test proposed copy or package changes with a large, representative sample

Don't let pricing erode a brand's value

Over the past two decades, a market structure has evolved which is more conducive to the use of price as a competitive tool. If a well-known, high quality brand is nurtured and sustained, it has true value to the consumer, who will be respectful of its premium price. Thus, marketers should avoid:

- Lowering a price to improve the brand's sales at the expense of its fundamental equity
- Using excessive price promotion as a means of encouraging the continued use of a weakening established brand

Maximize brand success on the shelf

How often do you go to a store to buy a particular product, such as Triscuits crackers, and find that, while there are 10 different varieties of Triscuits, your favorite, say "Original," is missing on the shelf? Marketers have done a disservice to their consumers with excessive product and brand proliferation. Not only does this unwarranted expansion erode brand loyalty, but it also leads to weaker sales of each brand in a portfolio. Companies' short-sighted efforts to gain more facings often lead them to ignore the way these additions will change the market structures at the most basic level – on the retail shelf. This often engenders price competition where none existed, and creates a more expensive method of marketing and production. In expanding its portfolio, smart marketers must:

- Constantly re-evaluate the brand's product assortment in terms of sizes, colors, formulations, flavors, etc., eliminating slow-moving items
- Maximize success at the retail level by focusing promotional support on the strongest brands in the line
- Build suggestions for retailers on which competitive item to "swap out" before any flanker or new product introductions

Build a strong relationship with the retailer

The emergence in the early part of this century of powerful retailers like Walmart and Target has changed the relationship between supplier and seller at the retail level. As Americans have become savvier, better-educated and more price-conscious consumers, the retail giants have been devoting sizeable promotion budgets to their own marketing activities. This has eroded traditional franchise-building advertising support for established brands and forced marketers to become more creative in their retail strategies. Here are a few suggestions for how a marketer can better access direct retail support for a brand:

- Move the trade away from a uniform schedule of price promotions to revenue-building merchandising activities
- Develop imaginative merchandising concepts which are chain-specific to replace generic promotions

Ensure advertising productivity in a crowded marketplace

During the "Mad Men" era, media plans were straightforward, often including a combination of network television advertising, printed media, in-store merchandising and even billboards. Don Draper could never have envisioned today's unstable, continually evolving media environment. Today more than ever, it is critical that marketers constantly reassess media expenditures in order to maximize advertising productivity. In developing advertising, brand managers and media planners should do the following:

- Focus creative efforts on maximizing message relevance, offer diversity in execution and maintain a tight strategic focus

- Use each medium in its most effective way; for example, broadcast for emotion, printed media for depth of information and social media for entertainment and awareness

- Ensure that every consumer demographic is reached by taking advantage of ever-changing communications media

Conduct a thorough strategic planning process

In my experience, companies today put too much emphasis on the formal elements of the planning process at the expense of real substance. In developing strategies for the future, rather than focusing on the current situation, marketers should identify the most material marketing issues the brand will face in the period ahead. It is critical to use the marketing planning process to guarantee optimum strategic oversight. It is also important to systematically evaluate brand performance based on specific objectives and strategies. Thus, in developing marketing plans, managers must:

- Use a situation analysis to forecast the future in the marketplace rather than focus on its history

- Review whether the strategies outlined in the marketing program are in fact being implemented

- Pay careful attention to how all resources are allocated: financial, analytical, physical and human

Conclusion

In the end, it is inevitable that the marketplace will continue to change – and smart marketers, who above all are committed to building and protecting strong brand identities, will successfully change with it.

In our next Lesson, we will build on the notion of **Brand Equity** by examining how marketers can use consumer research, which focuses on both psychological motivations and rigorous quantitative analysis, to identify a brand's unique market positioning – and thereby best assure its success in the marketplace.

Lesson 2:

Understanding consumer attitudes and behavior is fundamental to designing a meaningful brand strategy

"The aim of marketing is to know and understand the customer so well the product or service fits him and sells itself."

– Peter Drucker,
Father of Modern Management

Our first Lesson established the importance of building and protecting a strong brand identity. We laid out the process by which a marketer develops a specific brand, ensuring that it addresses a consumer need and that it has a meaningful point of difference versus its competition. In this second Lesson, we will explore the critical next step for market success: using consumer research to develop a brand strategy. We will see that, by undertaking carefully crafted, quantifiable market research, marketers can gain an in-depth understanding of how consumers feel and what motivates their purchase behavior.

In order to design a meaningful brand strategy, a marketer must answer several key questions: Who is my market target? What is my brand's promise or buying incentive? In laymen's terms, who are my ideal consumers and how do I convince them to buy my product? A review of the concept of market segmentation, along with an explication of a large-scale segmentation research methodology which I developed, will help guide us in answering these questions. I believe I will convince you that, if conducted properly, this research method is the best way to yield actionable information for developing a meaningful strategic positioning and generating positive results in the marketplace.

Market Segmentation

Over my six decades in the worlds of marketing and advertising, I had the privilege of studying and selling to consumers in over 75 different product categories, from peanut butter and cosmetics to automobiles and television sets. There is only one generalization about marketing I can make without fear of contradiction, and that is this: consumers are a diverse lot, with very different (almost infinitely varying) needs, abilities, interests and tastes, and therefore with very different desires for the products and services they seek.

While there are many ways to segment markets, the operative condition is to find the one variable most related to consumers' needs. Experience has shown that one of the variables most likely to work is ***Consumer Attitudes*** – since they are almost always related to consumer desires. In some product categories, however, usage behavior can be more important than attitudes. For a metal distributor, ***Usage Behavior*** – that is, whether you are a current heavy user, a current light user, a prior-user or a never-user of the brand – is what counts the most. In pet food, ***Product Usage*** is also critical – that is, whether you buy dry food, wet food or a mixture; whether you use food scraps or buy meat fresh from a butcher. For the most part, however, understanding ***Consumer Attitudes*** is the key to unlocking a brand's potential.

Our firm developed a novel methodology which showed that the best way to understand consumer attitudes and needs is to divide consumers into segments which articulate their unique characteristics. This, of course, requires considerable, and rather sophisticated, quantitative research, since you cannot guess as to how markets classify, how big the segments are and what their exact profiles will be.

Market segmentation, therefore, is fundamentally the operational approach by which a manufacturer caters to consumer diversity – by making product assortments that satisfy different consumer desires. It makes sense today because most markets are now so well penetrated that a few standard products will not satisfy everyone. Because markets are so big and widespread, manufacturers must use research to design products that can profitably be sold to an individual segment of the market.

But like everything else in our society, behavior moves like a pendulum, between extremes. Thus we have witnessed market behavior swing from too little to too much diversity. The proliferation of products has been so great that the resultant fragmentation of markets and marketing efforts has not only reduced corporate profits, but has also engendered considerable market failure. Where new market entries in the early 1950s had a success rate of over 80%, today that is the failure rate, and that percentage may well be increasing.

Classifying markets in terms of need

The basic problem for marketers, then, has become twofold: 1) How to identify the range of product diversity necessary to satisfy consumer desires, and 2) How to select those products which can most profitably cultivate that range of diversity.

These, unfortunately, are not easy problems to solve. What really makes them difficult is that the solutions vary by category. It is easy to recognize that what might be right for, say, pickles may be wrong for hosiery. As you can imagine, there is quite a difference between what consumers want in undergarments versus what they want to put on their hamburger. Obviously, the elements of their interest are far apart. But there are also major differences within each of these categories.

Beyond this challenge, we must also come to grips with how to classify each market in terms of its needs. Again, we face a complex task. To begin with, we now know that markets can be classified or segmented in many different dimensions.

Five key classifying dimensions

These are the five key dimensions that are usually considered in classifying needs. They are:

Demographics—The normal population characteristics: age, income, education, home ownership, or such things as skin color, body type and language.

Personality—The basic character and temperament of the individuals involved: whether they are authoritarian, narcissistic, permissive, and so on.

Lifestyle—The way people live, for example, whether they are sociable, active, home-oriented or vicarious. This is like personality but more behaviorally-oriented.

Purchasing behavior—The way people buy: whether they are heavy, light, prior or never-users; loyal to a brand or fickle; whether they shop a lot or rarely.

Product attitudes—How consumers feel toward a product in terms of what they want: whether they seek value, aesthetics, taste or prestige.

This last dimension, product attitudes, is the consumers' overt expression of need and therefore is often the most useful – particularly in those fields where the consumers can tell you rather specifically what will best gratify their desires. But this is not always the case. One must therefore be very careful not to choose what seems to be the most obvious need.

The operative principle in choosing the means for segmenting should be how relevant or correlated the classifying dimension is with consumer behavior. There are a number of ways of doing this. Needless to say, too many marketers have been guessing at it and have been wrong. For example, the number of toothpaste marketers who have convinced themselves that age is a basis for segmenting that market is legion. Yet, anyone who has studied the category systematically knows that product attributes and not age is the key classifying dimension. While some marketers have guessed that the education level of consumers plays a key role in the beer business, only those who have studied that business know that it is the uneducated man's liquor. Some who haven't done their research have made the mistake of believing personality or lifestyle is the key element in demand.

This is why I advocate using systematic market research to segment consumer behavior and attitudes. It will put you in the best position to truly understand the consumer and therefore to determine which overall strategic marketing actions make the most sense.

Market Segmentation Research

The key purpose of *Market Segmentation Research* is to determine if products are adequate for catering to various segments and if people in those segments can be persuaded to buy them. The only reliable way to be sure of the exact nature of that relationship is from direct knowledge of the consumer – what we in research call a consumer survey. The type and scope of the research used is extremely important – enough so that it is worth my spending some time on it.

In Lesson 4, I will enumerate the key criteria necessary for conducting scientifically-valid consumer research. For our current purposes, however, four points are worth emphasizing here:

1) Whatever you do must be quantified.

2) You must make sure you are getting a big enough sample to analyze the results by segment.

3) You must cover the full spectrum of needs in your questioning, that is, the consumer benefits, the consumer's ability to pay and the product's attributes.

4) You must cover the full spectrum of classification possibilities – demographics, personality, lifestyle, purchasing behavior and product attributes.

Permit me to again emphasize that, unless you have the appropriate data and analyze these data properly, you are bound to be disappointed. Let me also make one thing very clear. This is not inexpensive research. However, it is cheap in the sense that it can save you from the expense of market failure.

The real value of *Segmentation Research,* therefore, is quite simply this: It permits you to know your consumers directly and completely. In fact, it is the only truly valid consumer feedback mechanism you can count on in today's marketplace. What it does is permit you to return to the old one-on-one rudimentary sales situation – where national advertising is how you talk to consumers, and where market research is how consumers talk to you – how you learn about what they need and want, how they behave and feel, and who they really are.

Research Techniques

While I know most business executives are not interested in research methods, it is important to understand some aspects of the research techniques used to ascertain relevant market segments. Without getting into a lot of technical detail, you should know that the goals of *Segmentation Research* techniques are twofold.

The first goal is to determine what needs are associated with one another other. As we all know, there are many ways of saying the same thing. Therefore, our first task is to eliminate the duplication of phrases describing the same need and, in the process, ascertain which of them is important to consumers in evaluating products.

The second goal is to find out to what degree consumers in the population have similar need patterns. By doing this, we are in essence looking for groups of consumers with relatively homogeneous sets of needs which, if they exist, represent market segments.

Fortunately, both of these tasks are easily handled by a well-crafted market survey. Most of the time, the input can be of a verbal nature, that is, in terms of phrases like "It enhances my appearance," "It is comfortable to wear," or "It makes me feel important." However, when you are dealing with nuances in aesthetics, as is the case in tableware, you may have to use other approaches. For example, in classifying market segments in the silver flatware business, we used pictures very successfully.

But whatever technique is used, its primary purpose is, as I've said before, to determine operationally the most relevant basis for segmenting the market and then understanding it. This latter point is particularly important in marketing to a specific segment for, without having the characteristic data, you cannot truly understand it.

Strategic value of segmentation research

If conducted properly, **Segmentation Research** will very concretely help you in four strategic ways.

> 1) It will help you define your market target very precisely and accurately. Not only will you know what makes your target different from other segments of the market; you will also know what its demography, personality and lifestyle are.

2) It will permit you to know your competition and how best to address it. A good study will tell you where each market segment buys its merchandise, so you will even know against which channels of distribution you should place your emphasis in combating competition.

3) A good segmentation analysis will permit you to determine your best sources of business and will help you decide which are most worth going after. Since you will know the buying behavior of your segment, you can tell whether it makes the most sense to try to increase the incidence of use, the frequency of use or brand loyalty.

4) And finally, it will permit you to choose the best buying incentive for affecting your market target – that is, which benefits and attributes your item can support that will most likely elicit a positive response.

Author's Contribution:
The integration of psychological perceptions with quantitative analysis to identify consumers and define market segments

As we have established, the **Segmentation Study** is the use of quantitative methods to discern the appropriate market segments to go after and how best to motivate the consumers in those segments to buy a brand. It is by far the most sophisticated and complex means of acquiring communication feedback. It has merit in the case of unique and innovative products, but is essential for replacement and me-too products as well.

There are several valid market research techniques for determining segmentation. They include the N**eed/Satisfaction Study** and the **Consumer Acceptance Study.** In my experience, however, there is only one method which truly provides a large-scale, scientifically-valid path to accurate segmentation. And that is the *Market Target/Buying Incentive Study.*

Market Target/Buying Incentive Study

In the late 1960s, I helped develop an entirely new research methodology for segmenting consumer needs. I was working in the research department at *Grey Advertising* and one of our clients, the *Block Drug Company*, agreed to sponsor a major research project to help identify actionable business results. The study amassed data on consumer attitudes and purchase behavior. What was revolutionary about the technique was that it was not just testing concepts – it was an elaborate, quantitatively-based longitudinal study.

Fundamentally, the goal of the study was to assist marketers in using attitude and perception data to formulate a meaningful brand strategy. This, as you may recall, is exactly what we set out to do at the outset of this Lesson. The research design asked several key questions:

- Are consumers all the same – or do different segments of consumers have different needs?
- Is segmentation driven by attitude or behavior?
- Who are the most attractive target customers?
- What message will be most meaningful to them and make them willing to purchase a product over the competition?
- Are consumers' attitudes toward brands static, or are they susceptible to change?
- Do changes in consumers' attitudes cause changes in their buying behavior?

- If attitude changes influence behavior, do they produce parallel effects among both users and non-users of a brand?
- If attitudes influence behavior, what factors change a consumer's attitude? Is advertising one of them?
- Does product usage affect behavior as well?

It may seem strange to you that, in the 1960s, marketers hadn't yet asked these fundamental questions. But the market research industry was still young and its novel techniques were relatively unproven. Marketers had to be convinced of market research's validity – and that its strategic contributions merited its cost. In addition, many advertising professionals questioned whether the kind of attitude change that might occur toward a brand would be significant enough to be measured by available techniques.

Case Study: The Block Drug Company

Fortunately, we were able to convince the *Block Drug Company* to undertake a seminal segmentation study. With its uniquely-tailored design, the **Market Target/Buying Incentive Study** could determine definitively whether a relationship existed between consumers' attitudes and their purchasing behavior. It could also provide empirically-based observations to aid in our understanding of that relationship.

Test Design and Findings

Our firm conducted the study in three waves, among a probability sample of 2400 women in the United States. We contacted all 2400 subjects by telephone three times, three months apart in 1966, and asked them about 19 brands in 7 product categories: analgesics, cigarettes, coffee, denture cleaner, hair spray, mouthwash and peanut butter. The sample was large enough to generate a considerable amount of in-depth analysis.

The study produced extremely important information from which, after extensive statistical analysis, we concluded that:

1) Consumers hold attitudes about brands and express these attitudes in a consistent, measurable way.
2) Consumers' attitudes toward brands change constantly, even though on the surface they appear to remain fairly constant.
3) A consistently close relationship exists between attitudes and purchasing behavior.

Let's break these findings down. Our segmentation study revealed fascinating and somewhat surprising information about consumer attitudes and purchase behavior – as well as about the effectiveness of advertising. Here is a summary of our findings.

Consumer attitudes

- To maintain a brand's market position, the marketer must maintain a positive attitude among consumers. Even small attitude changes can unsettle them into becoming non-users.
- Some attributes are more influential than others in changing overall attitudes.

- Any attitude change alters the likelihood of future purchase. When a person's attitude toward a brand becomes favorable, the person is more likely to buy that brand.
- Even loyal users of a brand change their attitudes toward that brand at various times.
- Attitudes change more often among consumers who've never tried a brand than among those who've tried it in the recent or more remote past.

Purchase behavior

- Purchase behavior changes frequently, although less frequently than attitudes.
- If you are a satisfied user, you are more likely to purchase a brand again.
- Attitude data from two points in time can be used to predict a consumer's future purchase behavior in the third period with a high degree of accuracy.

Advertising exposure

- An advertising campaign which effectively communicates a brand's unique positioning versus its competition can change consumer attitudes.
- Frequent exposure to a brand's advertising results in measurably greater attitude change and a more positive attitude toward purchasing it.
- Effective advertising does more than just communicate information. It also persuades. It creates favorable attitudes toward a product and thereby increases the likelihood of purchase.

Some of these findings may seem obvious to you today, but they shook up the worlds of marketing and advertising at the time. There were many skeptics who did not believe that ***Market Target/Buying Incentive Study*** could be accurately applied to the development of an effective brand strategy or even an advertising execution. Fortunately, our firm developed sophisticated statistical scaling techniques for synthesizing the data and determining how the results could be applied to individual brands, as well as categories. The thoroughness of our research methods was compelling and, ultimately, convincing. The bottom line to you as a marketer today, of course, is that, if properly interpreted, this type of research can lead to the development of a meaningful brand strategy and, if well executed, will translate into business results in the marketplace.

Case Study: A Brand Positioning Statement

Now that we understand the value of ***Segmentation Research,*** we can reliably answer the issue we raised at the beginning of this Lesson: How to develop a better understanding of who the consumer is and what she wants. We now have the information we need to identify exactly who a brand's market target should be and which buying incentive will make that market target most likely to purchase a particular product. In other words, we can create its ***Brand Positioning Statement.***

Perhaps the best way to illustrate how this learning can be practically applied is to provide an example. In this case, we will use a hypothetical shampoo product called Spree. Let us say you are a member of the marketing team which has just completed an in-depth segmentation study on your brand, Spree. You are ready to begin developing a meaningful brand strategy for the product. For simplicity's sake, in demonstrating this process, we will insert some assumptions about what the learning from the segmentation study revealed.

There are four key components to developing a **Brand Positioning Statement** for Spree Shampoo. Let's identify each component and then review the relevant information contributed by the Spree study.

Component 1: Who is the market target?

Which consumer should you be going after? Whose attitudes and behavior make them pre-disposed to buying your product? In the case of Spree, it turns out to be young women who want healthy, shiny hair.

Market target: Spree is the hair care brand for women 18-25 who want to look beautiful and are concerned about the health of their hair.

Component 2: What is the buying incentive?

What are you offering to your target consumer? What is the meaningful benefit that she will get if she buys your brand? What is the differentiated offering which you are providing and the competition is not? Everyone wants beautiful hair: How does your brand deliver it in a way that consumers care about? In the case of our research, the most compelling perceived benefit of Spree was its pro-vitamin aspect.

Buying incentive: Spree gives you healthy, beautiful hair because of its pro-vitamin formula.

Component 3: What is the source of business?

Who is your brand competing against? Is it a product category (all shampoos) or a more specific usage segment (high-end shampoos)? Our research found that Spree users were most likely to be women who were open to switching from a higher-priced brand which was failing to deliver on one of its claimed product attributes, shine.

Source of business: Users of a higher-priced shampoo which overpromises on the attribute of shine.

Component 4: What is the brand personality?

How would you describe the brand in terms of human characteristics? What is its tone of voice? What personality elements could you build into the brand's communications?

Brand Personality: The Spree consumer is attractive, outgoing and concerned about her appearance.

Brand Positioning Statement for Spree Shampoo

Now let's put all the components of the brand positioning together.

> Spree is the hair care brand for women 18-25 who want to look beautiful and are concerned about the health of their hair. Spree gives you healthy, beautiful hair because of its pro-vitamin formula. The consumers most likely to purchase Spree are users of a higher-priced shampoo which overpromises on shine. The Spree consumer is attractive, outgoing and concerned about her appearance.

So, now we have developed a very precise **Brand Positioning Statement** for our product. By using reliable information carefully gleaned from our large-scale **Market Segmentation Study,** we now understand clearly which consumers are predisposed to purchase our brand and what will motivate their purchase behavior. This unique brand positioning can now be translated into a detailed and actionable **Strategic Marketing Plan.**

Segmentation Research in the Marketplace

Before we leave the subject of **Market Segmentation Research,** I would like to provide two examples of studies which our consulting firm performed for clients in the wake of the *Block Drug Company* study. Over the years, our firm refined the methodology for the **Market Target/Buying Incentive Study** and, as technology improved, we established even more sophisticated approaches to pinpointing how consumer attitudes can be translated to a **Brand Positioning Statement.** Here are two good examples of how a segmentation study changed the thinking behind the way a brand was being positioned – and improved the brand's performance in the marketplace. As you will see, the key to the success of these studies was that they were designed to address the very specific strategic questions at hand.

Case Study: Hanes Hosiery

In the late 1980s, the marketing team for *Hanes Hosiery* asked our firm to identify the key motivator for purchase of their basic hosiery brand. The team believed that income was the key determinant of desire – that the Hanes brand's consumers had a higher than average income. In fact, the segmentation study showed that this was not the case. It turned out that attitudes, not income, were the primary agent motivating purchase.

The segmentation study identified five segments in the hosiery category, each with a unique set of desires. Because we used a large sample of women, we were able to tell just how big each segment was. What we discovered was that the Hanes brand was considered by consumers to be in the "fashion" segment of the category. As its name suggests, the people in the "fashion" segment were more interested in the stylistic and aesthetic elements of hosiery and less concerned with support properties. Moreover, their general attitudes toward hosiery reflected this fashion orientation.

When we checked the personality traits of the "fashion" segment, we found that they were very much related to attitudes. Consumers interested in the Hanes brand tended to be more narcissistic and exhibitionistic than consumers in the other segments. Next we looked at the demographics of this group. They were essentially somewhat younger and more likely to be employed, but – critically – they did not turn out to be as high on the income scale as the marketing team had previously assumed. Finally, we looked at brand behavior. We found that this segment had a greater propensity than others to buy a branded entry.

The conclusion for the Hanes marketing team, therefore, was that they needed to make a change to the brand's positioning to capitalize on the target consumer's attitudes toward the brand. The new positioning focused on the fashion properties of the brand. Not surprisingly, this change was successful in reaching the target consumer and resulted in increased sales of the product.

Case Study: Clairol Hair Care

While the Hanes example illustrates the role that **Segmentation Research** can play in identifying the optimum market target, another example shows how this type of test can pinpoint a brand's source of business. In the 1990s, the management at *Clairol Hair Care* asked our firm to test the marketing team's hypothesis that the primary source of business for its mid-priced color line was new users. Sources of business can include any or all of the following types of consumers: 1) current consumers making incremental purchases, 2) consumers who are currently buying a competitor, or 3) new users entering the market for the first time.

Prior to the national study, *Clairol* had been focusing its marketing efforts for this secondary mid-priced product line on attracting non-users into the market, using a strong generic selling theme. Based on what we learned in the research, the team subsequently changed its strategic efforts to appeal directly to users of the market leader by employing a direct-competitive theme.

What the research clearly showed was that resistance to the use of hair color among non-users was strongly entrenched, and these consumers would not likely yield to this resistance based on the small advertising weight this secondary brand could afford. The research also revealed areas of dissatisfaction among users of the leading hair color brand, in terms of both imagery and supportable functional product attributes. Thus, there appeared to be an opportunity to reposition the secondary brand in a way that would address consumers' perceptions of the attribute deficits in the leading brand. Needless to say, repositioning this secondary brand to target this new source of business had a very positive effect on its sales – a repositioning that the manufacturer was originally reluctant to take without strong quantitative evidence to support it.

Clearly, the *Market Target/Buying Incentive* research had real value for both the Hanes and Clairol brands. It allowed the marketers to redefine their brand's positioning, and to more accurately address the needs and behavior of the most likely consumers of the products. This was not the first time that market segmentation research surprised and impressed a client and led to improved business performance. Importantly to me, it also helped raise the estimation of quantitative segmentation research as the valuable tool it is considered today.

Conclusion

As we end our discussion of brand strategy, I hope that I have communicated the groundbreaking importance of the *Market Target/Buying Incentive* research I pioneered. My specific contribution – the integration of psychological considerations with quantitative analysis to identify consumers and define market segments – is even more valued in our increasingly diverse and competitive environment today.

We are now ready to move on to our next Lesson, where we will learn how to translate a meaningful brand strategy into a detailed *Strategic Marketing Plan.* As always, our aim is to strengthen a brand's identity, as well as to reap rewards in the broader marketplace.

Lesson 3:

Keeping up with an ever-changing marketplace requires disciplined strategic marketing planning

"Planning is fundamentally an intellectual process and a mental disposition to do things in an orderly way, to think before acting, and to act in light of facts rather than guesses."

– Lyndall Urick,
Economics Philosopher

You might think that by now we have done the hard part – we have built a strong brand with a meaningful strategic positioning – and identified who our target consumer is and what will motivate her to purchase our product. In fact, all of this good work is in vain if we do not take the critical next step – transforming this solid base into marketing success via a disciplined **Strategic Marketing Planning Process.**

To briefly review, in our first Lesson, we established the importance of building and protecting a strong brand identity. We laid out the process by which a marketer develops a specific brand, ensuring that it addresses a consumer need and that it has a meaningful point of difference vs. its competition. In Lesson 2, we saw that understanding consumer perceptions of a product's value – gained through carefully crafted research – is fundamental to designing an effective brand strategy. Now we are ready for our third Lesson, where we will articulate the process by which a strong brand proposition can be converted to an actionable strategic plan which will lead to positive business results.

Before we begin, a reminder that, for simplicity's sake, I will be using the term "product" or "brand" to refer to all types of brands, be they goods, services or retail establishments.

Author's Contribution: The development of a systematic strategic marketing planning process

I am proud to say that it is at the very beginning of this Lesson on **Strategic Marketing Planning** that I can identify our firm's important contribution to the marketing industry. This is because we were among the first market researchers to articulate the role of a **Strategic Marketing Planning Process** in achieving business success. Once again, I am grateful to a visionary business leader for suggesting that we tackle a critical unanswered question. In this case, the question was: Can a marketer develop a systematic approach to strategic planning for a specific brand? As we all know today, the answer is quite definitively yes.

While the term *Strategic Marketing* is integral to the mission of every brand-oriented company, the concept is not as old as you'd think. As I've mentioned before, I strongly believe that the vision of senior management is critical to success in any business. This became clear to me back in 1974, when the CEO of *Alcan Aluminum* approached our firm. At the time, *Alcan* was a production-oriented company which primarily manufactured house siding. Thus it was quite unusual – and innovative – for him to ask us to facilitate a two-day seminar for 24 senior executives on how to prepare a marketing plan. It was such a novel concept that we found ourselves having to define many new terms.

The CEO participated throughout the process, no doubt in part to impress upon his staff that he was serious about its purpose. But his presence underscored for me the value of management buy-in to marketing success, which I outlined in Lesson 1. In more general terms, the experience helped our firm create a model which we then used to develop strategic plans for many companies over the years, including *IBM, Sara Lee* and *Nationwide Insurance*. Below is an overview of what we ultimately created – a comprehensive template for the **Strategic Marketing Planning Process**.

The Value of Marketing Planning

The value of marketing planning – which, if properly executed, is a great deal of work – cannot be underestimated. What planning does is force you to think about your business conceptually. It makes you consider your competition more thoroughly; it uncovers problems and unearths exploitable opportunities. Planning ensures that all of a company's resources, both physical and intellectual, are brought to bear on its marketing activities with maximum utility. And finally, it minimizes uncertainty by anticipating change.

The value of marketing planning to executive management should be obvious. First of all, it provides a precise description of the business situation the company will have to face. It identifies the specific revenue and profit objectives it can expect, the decisions necessary to accomplish them, and the premises upon which they are based. Most important, the end result of the planning process will be a reference document against which both to check current activity and to evaluate past performance. Strategic planning keeps the long-range view in mind, thus avoiding short-sighted, purely opportunistic actions, which are often counterproductive. And finally, it permits the executive in charge to hold individuals accountable for their decisions and actions.

The Strategic Marketing Plan

Fundamentally, **Strategic Marketing Planning** is the business process that a company uses:

1) To systematically evaluate the market situation it will face in the future.

2) To establish specific marketing objectives, in both revenue and profit terms, that it hopes to achieve in the marketplace.

3) To draft and implement detailed marketing programs and activities for accomplishing its objectives, based on sound strategies.

4) To allocate the resources needed to implement the programs and activities.

5) To control and measure the results of the marketing programs so that they are consistently implemented and evaluated against the approved marketing strategy.

There are four steps to developing a *Strategic Marketing Plan*: 1) Undertaking a thorough *Marketing Analysis,* 2) Creating the *Marketing Plan* document, 3) Taking the *Marketing Plan* to the marketplace and 4) Evaluating the *Marketing Plan's* effectiveness.

Planning is the hardnosed work in the home office that instructs the implementers on which marketing activities they should focus on, based on a realistic and relevant analysis of the market situation. Implementing is the hardnosed work on the firing line to make sure that the programs are executed, sales are made, the goods are delivered, the receipts are collected and the customers are kept satisfied. Both are critical to an effective, efficient operation.

Step 1: Undertake a Market Analysis

The first step in developing a *Strategic Marketing Plan* is to use analytical techniques to assess the market situation. This will tell you where your brand stands today and what you need to know about the future in terms of the marketplace. The *Market Analysis* is essentially an analytical description, backed by all of the available relevant facts about the current environment and the marketing forces affecting it. It describes the situation that the company and its competitors will be facing over the period covered by the plan. In Lesson 4, I will outline in detail the various types of research which help facilitate this type of analysis.

There are several key components of the *Market Analysis,* including: 1) Understanding consumer attitudes, 2) Assessing the competitive situation, and 3) Reviewing the brand's current strength against several functional areas, such as pricing, trade activity and marketing communications. In addition, some broader, non-brand related situations, such as the economic marketplace and the availability of corporate resources, should be reviewed.

The Brand Review

A *Strategtic Markeing Plan* should always begin with a thorough *Brand Review*.

Any respectable *Marketing Analysis* should begin with the consumer. Using different research techniques, the team can evaluate how well its brand is positioned to generate sales, i.e., to be chosen by the consumer over the competition. Specific questions to be asked include: 1) Does the brand have attributes that resonate with the market target – such matters as durability, value, convenience, appearance and pride? 2) Is the brand's equity, in total or considering its individual attributes – such as awareness, familiarity, predilection for purchase and brand loyalty – powerful enough to help the brand generate incremental profitable revenue?

Assess the competitive situation

It is equally critical to conduct a review of your brand in terms of how well it stacks up against the products or brands with which it competes for consumer sales – that is, the competitive set. Where does your product fit in the *Basic Brand Asset Model* outlined in Lesson 1? How well does it perform against the competition in terms of the four features: *Product, Marketing, Brand* and *Management Equities*? Is your brand adequately differentiated from its competitors in a relevant manner, or must it be changed to make it more distinctive?

Review key functional areas

A detailed evaluation of the product in terms of the key functional areas is also an essential step to assessing a brand's viability. The functional areas are all of the ways that the company works together to get the product to the shelf. These include: product development, sales, distribution, packaging, marketing communications, pricing and, lastly, logistics. It often makes sense to interview key people in marketing and sales about what they see as impediments to these functions, since they are the ones closest to the day-to-day business.

Here is just a sample of questions about different functional areas which the market analysis should ask:

1) Is the brand effectively using price, trade margins, guarantees, warranties and credit terms as competitive tools?

2) Does the brand's market power permit it to obtain a premium price, or should it be sold at the market price or at a discount?

3) Does the trade have an appreciation for the brand's value and is the brand maximizing its potential at the retail level?

4) What is the ideal advertising mix in terms of consumer, trade, online, product publicity, sponsorship and in-store merchandising?

5) Is there an opportunity to expand the brand's geographical reach – locally, regionally, nationally or globally?

Once the brand has been carefully analyzed in terms of consumer perceptions, the competitive situation and the product's functional strengths, a few non-brand related issues should be explored.

Analyze the economic marketplace

The first non-brand related task is an assessment of factors occurring in the general economy, such as GDP, the rate of inflation, interest rates and employment – and their potential impact. Also, the team should review the status of legislative issues and technological changes that could affect the plan. In each case, forecasts of the future should be prepared. These are factors that could affect demand, as well as consumer and trade attitudes.

Identify internal or corporate issues

Every brand's plan should assess how well the resources of the company can and will support it. All plans require some type of financial investment. It's important to assess management's attitude toward the specific brand and its willingness to commit the resources needed to make the desired overall profit. In addition, a careful planner should consider existing policies and traditions of the company which could prove to be either impediments or incentives for action.

Explore external opportunities

Finally, a marketing plan's development occasionally coincides with the rise of new opportunities available in the company, which it can feasibly exploit. These can include new categories the company is now competent to enter, new territories it is not in, new channels of distribution or an increased emphasis on spending, to name a few possibilities.

Step 2: Create the Marketing Plan document

Once the thorough *Market Analysis* of the brand is complete, the marketing team should be equipped with a solid understanding of where the product stands versus the competition, how the product can best be marketed in the year ahead, what specific strategic and financial goals are achievable and what is the best way to achieve them. Once again, the term "product" is intended to refer to branded items across all industries.

It is then time to develop the specific *Strategic Marketing Plan*. There are three key elements to the plan: 1) **Objectives** or overall goals, 2) **Strategies** or specific targets, and 3) **Tactics,** which are specific actions implemented in the marketplace to facilitate the achievement of the plan.

Marketing Objectives

Quite simply, *Marketing Objectives* describe, in specific transactional terms, where the team wants the brand to be in the future. The objectives are an explicit statement of the unit sales expectations, revenue expectations and profit expectations that the marketing program is designed to achieve in the timeframe covered by the plan – and for each product and brand in the product line. *Marketing Objectives* include marketing investment objectives as well.

Marketing Strategies

Once the *Marketing Objectives* have been determined, the brand team must spell out how they will be executed across all of the functional areas. This activity is called the *Marketing Strategies* and should address all aspects of getting a product into the hands of the consumer.

Marketing Tactics

And finally, the team must develop *Marketing Tactics,* which is where marketing, like a tire, hits the road. The tactics refer to what is actually done in marketplace. They are essentially a translation of strategic objectives into specific logistical and tactical actions. Many have said that tactics are what it's all about. That is only partially true, as we know that strategy is always key. Yet, well executed tactics directly affect what will happen in terms of both revenue and profit.

Case Study: A Sample Marketing Plan

Perhaps it will be helpful now to provide an example of how the three key elements of a plan – *Objectives, Strategies and Tactics* – could be applied to a specific product. Let's return to Spree, our hypothetical shampoo from Lesson 2. You will recall that we were positioning Spree as a shampoo with a unique pro-vitamin formula which appeals to women 18-25 who are dissatisfied with a more expensive competitive product.

Therefore, one element of Spree's marketing plan might look like this:

Objective: To increase Spree's brand share

Strategy: To attract new users from the competition via a new communications plan

Tactic: To run an advertising campaign on national television targeted against women 18-25 who want healthy, beautiful hair

So, you can see that we have identified one specific objective for the plan – in terms of Spree's brand share – as well as the strategies and tactics required to execute that objective. The marketing team would then proceed to create objectives, strategies and tactics for the other key elements of the plan, such as revenue, profit and unit sales.

Once the monumental task of articulating the **Strategic Marketing Plan** is completed, there is much more work ahead. In my experience, the success of a marketing plan requires the cooperation and coordination of all of the functional areas supporting a brand. And having in place a disciplined, focused and motivated management team is key to making that happen.

Step 3: Take the Plan to the marketplace

The implementation of a **Strategic Marketing Plan** is simply the actual execution of all the activities it entails. If the development of the objectives and strategies for the marketing plan were based on a thoughtful, conscientious incorporation of the important learning gained from the **Marketing Analysis,** it follows that putting the plan itself into place should be a lay-up. Not so. The successful execution of a marketing plan depends upon an obsessive attention to detail, which means that every member of the marketing team must work to the best of their ability to execute those activities in the marketplace as efficiently and effectively as possible.

Case Study: Failure to Execute a Plan

Over the years, our firm conducted a number of research and strategic projects for the *Ryerson Company,* America's biggest metal distributor. One experience in particular showed me the critical importance of successful marketing plan implementation. In 1980, our firm completed a three-year strategic marketing planning process for *Ryerson.* In the first two years of the plan, the business met or even exceeded expectations in terms of both sales and profits. But in the third year, the results were quite disappointing. To understand why, we conducted a thorough review of how the specific tactics we had developed had been implemented. What we discovered was that the people executing those tactics had fallen short on several key dimensions, including missing distribution targets and failing to execute price rollbacks.

Intrigued by the *Ryerson* experience, our firm went back and analyzed the results in the marketplace for several of the strategic plans which we had delivered to other major companies. While most plans had met with success, a few of them failed to meet expectations. Upon further study we found that, in large part, the plans failed because the people implementing them did not effectively translate strategic directives into tactical actions. Interestingly, in some cases, the plans failed because those who implemented the plan actually subverted the actions since they didn't agree with them or had a different agenda.

In order to address the disappointing results in the *Ryerson* case, we quickly put together a system for operationalizing the marketing plan which we had developed for the business for the coming year. We created a process whereby the implementation of the strategy could be directly translated into specific human activities. We met with people in key functional areas across the company, identified the specific tasks which were required to achieve every component of the strategic plan, and assigned specific individuals to those tasks. If the company staff was lacking a particular expertise, we identified an alternate source of manpower. For example, we discovered that the promotional program that we had recommended could not be implemented without the help of an outsourced full-service marketing communications agency. Within six weeks, we had hired an agency and they were working, in concert with the rest of the marketing team, to implement the company's strategic marketing plan in the marketplace – with positive business results.

Step 4: Evaluate the Plan's effectiveness

As we have seen, harnessing a talented team to execute the details of a strategic plan in the marketplace is critical. However, it is not always a guarantee of success. The term *Marketing Controls* describes one of the major disconnects in business – that is, the difference between what is planned and what gets done. In order to assure success, it is necessary for the planners to designate some marketing controls, which are procedures to reassure management that the plan is being carried out as it was originally conceived and that the plan's objectives are being met.

To do this requires two things: management oversight and quantifiable marketing milestones. Management oversight involves periodic meetings to assess what is actually taking place in the marketplace. Marketing milestones can include a variety of data tools.

Measure business results

One of the best ways to evaluate a plan's results is to use sales and profits as *Measurements*. After all, the aim of marketing is to generate revenue, and there is no better measure of this than unit transactions, or sales, and the profits achieved by them. While the total numbers are important, more can be learned by insightful analysis, which becomes critical if the results are unexpectedly negative. Suffice it to say that breaking the numbers down by product category, brands, sizes, flavors, price points, geographical areas, customers, outlets and time periods can explain a great deal. The aim of this type of analysis should always be to seek the causes of any changes versus the plan and to ascertain whether the difficulties, if there are any, are the result of strategic, logistical or tactical shortcomings. Obviously, the next critical step is to identify how those shortcomings can be addressed.

Ask the consumer

A second marketing control is *Tracking Studies.* These usually take the form of consumer surveys which measure buying behavior, usage and attitudes toward the product, the brand and the company. Customer satisfaction studies are a form of tracking research that can be extremely useful. A few years after our firm did the strategic work for the *Ryerson Company*, the management asked us to conduct a Tracking Study to determine exactly why metal distributors are selected. It turned out that a customers' choice of a metal distributor was a mirror image of what dissatisfied them. We called the selection criteria the "Big 5." Or survey showed that the Big 5 reasons for choosing a distributor essentially reflected the services – not the product – they provided: 1) a competitive price, 2) the availability of inventory, 3) delivery on time when the product is needed, 4) a speedy price quote, and 5) an order delivered in perfect condition.

While *Ryerson* believed it was selling metal, it was really selling its services as a provider of the metal that a customer wanted to buy. They began using the "Big 5 Factors" as the strategic incentive, including them in sales material, advertising and promotions. I am happy to report that the firm turned around its sales, produced enough profits to raise its stock price 200% and was able to buy a major competitor.

Test the Plan in the marketplace

A third evaluative measure for a plan's success is *In-Market Testing.* By dividing the total market into equal and similar groups of smaller units, and by varying individual elements of a plan in different areas of the country, it is possible to discern which of the marketing plan's elements are most effective. I used this method with one of my clients, *H&R Block,* which sells income tax preparation services. I will describe this approach in detail in the next Lesson.

Assess the financial results

Finally, and especially important in today's financially-focused business environment, a plan should be evaluated in terms of a company's **Return on Investment.** This measurement is composed of two variables. The first relates to the plan's ability to generate revenue. The second is the cost or investment made to achieve the plan's goals.

Conclusion

As a final note on marketing planning, I'd like to reinforce the role of management in affecting change. A key element of the successful implementation of a marketing plan is the willingness on the part of management to allow revisions. Once it becomes obvious that the company's expectations for a business are not being met, changes should be made to the degree that such changes are possible. This can become clear at many points in the planning cycle, even in the early implementation. If a plan is falling short of its objectives – in terms of sales or profits – wise management will resist pulling financial support from the business. Instead, it will direct the brand team to make revisions to the plan and, if they seem both strategically and financially sound, it will authorize them.

Now that we have established how to develop a ***Strategic Marketing Plan,*** we will move on to a discussion of one of the most critical elements of the planning process. In our next Lesson, we will review in detail the nuts and bolts of conducting scientifically-valid and actionable ***Marketing Research.***

Lesson 4:

The application of science to marketing makes brand management more professional and improves results

"Without measurement we do not have science."

– Lord Thomas Kelvin, Scottish Mathematician

The first three Lessons of this book have led us inevitably to our next topic: the critical role that science plays in the development of sound **Strategic Marketing Planning** and, ultimately, business results.

In Lesson 1, we saw that constructing a research-based **Basic Brand Asset Model** guides the creation of a strong brand identity. Lesson 2 showed how understanding consumer attitudes and purchase behavior is key to articulating a meaningful **Brand Positioning Statement.** And finally, Lesson 3 illustrated the important role disciplined situation analysis plays in developing an actionable *Strategic Marketing Plan*. Now we are ready to tackle the specific and myriad types of qualitative and quantifiable *Market Research* which substantively inform these processes.

Time and again over the course of my career, I have seen that the application of science to marketing makes marketing more professional. This is because commercial *Market Research*, when it is conducted properly, provides two key inputs for management. First, it helps identify business opportunities. Second, it helps reduce business risk. Well-executed, scientifically-based research should therefore be a critical element of the decision-making process at all levels of a company's planning. In fact, if management effectively applies sound market research to the implementation of its over-arching objectives, that research is guaranteed to play a key role in business success.

In Lesson 4, we will explore in more depth the role that different types of market research play in the development and refinement of a brand's positioning and marketing plan. We've already outlined how attitude research with consumers is a vital part of strategic planning. Now we will review other types of research, including *Focus Groups, Copy* and *Product Tests,* and research both in stores and in the actual marketplace. We will identify how these tests can be tailored to answer specific strategic and tactical questions. We will also see how, once a plan is implemented, research can help marketers examine the core elements of that plan in the marketplace – and ensure that the plan is on-track and that resources are being maximized.

Market Research: An Overview

When I joined *McCann-Erickson* in 1957, market research was in its infancy. As a member of the newly created research department, I saw that our task was to convince both the agency management and, subsequently, the client that, if the correct quantitative methods were applied, **Market Research** could drive the development of a more effective brand strategy. This is, of course, commonly acknowledged today. It seems that even the most skeptical executives understand that, while judgment is important in any process, the value of rigorous testing and proving hypotheses cannot be underestimated.

As we begin this discussion, it is important to point out that market research is an extremely broad field and that some methods are more effective – and scientifically valid – than others. I'd like to provide a brief review of the purpose of market research and then outline some of the most important quantitative and qualitative forms. I will conclude this exposition with a detailed review of the **Checkerboard Test,** a test which I originated and which I believe was my most important contribution to the field of market research. It is my hope that this Lesson will give you a clear understanding of what can be expected from market research, how it should be designed and used for maximum impact, and the critical need to avoid misusing it as a tool.

Before we begin reviewing the specific types of research, I'd like to re-emphasize the importance of applying science to the process. Simply put, if you are going to do research, make sure it is good. It should be carefully designed to address the specific business question at hand. It should respect scientific conditions. For test results to be meaningful, they must include very large samples which are representative of the national or regional marketplace in which the brand is competing.

In my years of experience, I have learned that adhering to these rules is the best way to test any proposition – and that tests of an actual idea or product in the marketplace are the most effective. Having said that, there is a place for less scientific, but nevertheless predictive research. Some questions, such as whether an early product concept idea should be further explored, can be answered with a small **Concept Test**. For the most part, however, the best outcomes are naturally derived from the best input.

Design methodology

Designing quantitative research so that it predicts a national outcome is not as simple as some marketers believe. The devil we are fighting is **Market Variation,** which is inherent in the marketplace. While it is generally recognized that a large number of variables can affect sales performance – variables such as price, availability, competition, weather and economic conditions – it is often tacitly assumed in market research that, if these variables are ignored, they will not cause any trouble. Or, to be more precise, it is assumed that these variables are randomly distributed and that the effect of each will be canceled out in the total. But this prediction is, at best, an optimistic hope with any research method. To assume that results are actionable when tests do not account for the various market variables is wishful thinking.

As with any laboratory experiment, there are three **Methodological Conditions** which I believe yield the best results in quantitative research:

1) The experiment or test must be representative of the whole. It must be possible to translate the results to the real-world marketplace.

2) The test must be carefully controlled. One must do what is planned and keep extraneous variables from contaminating the test. This is particularly important in testing alternative variables, where a control group against which the new element can be compared is necessary.

3) The test must be accurately measured. This is a much more complex issue than usually supposed. For one thing, which type of sales measure should be used – factory shipments, retail sales or consumer usage? Even after accepting a measurement criterion, there is the matter of projecting it to the total. There are many methods for doing this, and they often yield different answers. There is also the issue of the base period against which the comparison is to be made, and there are various approaches to this as well.

I should note here that there is probably nothing which can disrupt a test from being predictive more than extraneous noise. No matter how carefully we control test inputs, unless the external variables are kept under control, prediction is virtually impossible. Variation has traditionally been dealt with in one of three ways: by ignoring it, by attempting to match markets, or by using the statistical principles of experimental design.

Use of research in strategic marketing planning

Now that we've established the optimum *Methodological Conditions,* we will move on to how *Market Research* is applied in the strategic planning and implementation process. As we saw in Lesson 3, a plan developed for a specific brand focuses on a one-year period. But obviously, planning should be a continuous exercise. While a plan is being executed, its leaders should be conducting ongoing research to confirm that the plan is effective. They should always be exploring, testing and evaluating other ideas or aspects of the plan to improve it for the coming year – or even to make revisions mid-year. For example, if research shows that a media program in place is not reaching the right consumers, the media plan should be modified as soon as those results are in.

Here is a brief summary of how marketers can use research directly in the strategic planning process:

- To collect and review available research to help with the planning. Both primary and secondary data are useful.
- To develop a one-year strategic plan based on studies of specific tactics: which advertising to use, how much to spend, etc.
- To conduct ongoing research to study the effectiveness of a plan's key variables.
- To adjust a plan for the next year based on new learning – or to make mid-year revisions if the research warrants it.

Obviously, the strategic, logistical and tactical decisions marketers make are based on addressing a particularly complex and dynamic market of great diversity. Until the decisions are implemented in the marketplace, we really do not know whether they will actually work. The fact is that human behavior – especially when it comes to financial transactions – is very difficult to predict. Hence we need some systematic method of measurement to help make informed guesses. Fortunately, we have a number of techniques for doing this.

Primary and secondary research

There are two types of research which are useful in predicting consumer behavior: primary and secondary. In this Lesson, we will review several examples of each. **Primary Research** is direct research conducted by the marketer. This includes **Market Surveys** of consumer behavior and attitudes and **Tracking Studies,** such as brand awareness and usage tests. It also includes **Single Market Tests** conducted in the marketplace of proposed new advertising, products or packages.

Secondary Research is the collection of material that already exists, which others make available for general use. This includes syndicated market data, such as a scan of sales in a category. These data are purchased from companies like *Nielsen* or *IRI,* but there are also many untapped free sources of valuable data. An array of government statistics – from the various censuses and specialized studies used in national accounting – can be extremely instructional. Business associations, investment houses and private firms produce a variety of meaningful and accessible market reports. Closer to home, what is often not mined are a company's internal files, which may include survey data, as well as sales data and other materials that can be extremely useful in planning.

So you see that **Secondary Research** features data produced elsewhere, while **Primary Research** is developed at the discretion and under the direction of marketing managers. The best of these managers oversees the design of **Primary Market Research Studies** to carefully answer the strategic question at hand. This requires using an analytical framework that leads to an accurate understanding of what motivates consumers' purchase decisions, which can then be translated into actual business results.

Using research to answer strategic questions

There are many strategic questions across all the elements of the marketing mix which research can help answer to determine if a brand strategy is being communicated effectively. Here are some examples:

- Which ad should I use?
- Am I communicating my brand positioning in the right way?
- Is my copy effective?
- Does my product best meet my target consumer's need?
- Is my packaging effective?
- Am I spending the right amount of money?
- Is my media mix correct?
- Am I successfully achieving my financial business results?

For obvious reasons, this last question – Is the strategic plan getting the desired business results? – is most important for management. There are many measurements which can be used to answer the question of strategic results: growth in brand share, sales per store, satisfaction levels based on consumer surveys and increased distribution in the marketplace. As you'll see, there are also many different methods for attempting to answer this question.

Types of Market Research

We will now turn to a description of the various types of *Primary Market Research.* This review will begin with those methods which I believe are least reliable and will move to the ones which take place in the marketplace – and which I believe best guide marketers in evaluating the effectiveness of a *Strategic Marketing Plan.* Specifically, you will see that those methods which can address specific market variables in a controlled situation will best determine if a brand's positioning is on target, and if a strategic plan is maximizing its return on marketing investment.

Please note that in this Lesson, I will not be discussing the type of market research outlined in Lesson 2. As you'll recall, Lesson 2 illustrated in detail how the use of a psychological exploration of attitudes and behavior, paired with quantitative analysis, allows marketers to identify their brand's consumers and to define specific market segments. I hope that by now it is obvious how this form of research, particularly the *Market Target/Buying Incentive Study,* is fundamental to designing a meaningful **Brand Positioning Statement.**

I will now review the different types of tests in the order in which I believe they have scientific legitimacy. Where relevant, I will provide examples of how our firm used these methods in conducting research for companies, including *Procter & Gamble* and *H&R Block,* for whom we designed the **Checkerboard Test.**

Focus Groups

Qualitative research, when first established in the 1950s, was designed to help marketers understand why people behave the way they do. Its aim was to elucidate how beliefs and attitudes affect consumer behavior. A variety of techniques were developed, including small sample motivation surveys and in-depth one-on-one interviews. Today the field is dominated by the use of *Focus Groups.*

Focus Groups consist of small-sample, intensive interview process. There are typically 10-12 consumers in a group, who have been recruited based on criteria such as relevant product use, age, ethnicity, or socio-economic level. Ideally, the group is representative of the brand's target market. A trained moderator exposes the group to a product idea or a physical product itself and probes the participants for their reactions – both conscious and subconscious. The moderator focuses on the question which the research has been designed to answer. For example, for an existing brand it might be, "Do you think this change represents a product improvement?" or, for a new product, "Would you be interested in trying it?" The question is typically asked in several different ways to provide richer data for analysis. The more sophisticated studies also use some projective techniques to identify the personality traits that may underlie possible product usage.

It is my contention that Focus Groups are the least reliable form of market research. Fundamentally, because the method is not data-based, it does not adhere to the scientific tenets outlined in our discussion of methodology above. The participants are randomly chosen and usually located in only one or two markets, and the sample sizes are not big enough to be representative of any relevant group. The analysis is perforce highly subjective. The conclusions, therefore, do not constitute predictive or projectable research.

Having said that, I must acknowledge that, while Focus Groups should never be used for concrete decision-making, they can be helpful for exploratory purposes. It is always good for marketers to hear directly from consumers about how they view a particular product and perceive its broader competitive category. Further, early in a new product's development, initial reactions to potential brand names or preliminary package designs can be instructive. Nevertheless, Focus Group results should never be used to make either strategic or tactical decisions. Rather they should be used as a guide and to help refine more scientific research.

Market Survey

A *Market Survey* is a rudimentary form of primary research which provides a randomized sample of data about either a particular product or service. Market Surveys can include consumer purchase studies, trade attitude assessments and audits of sales or distribution. Market Surveys are important in marketing planning, because they offer a considerable amount of data about the buyers, the sellers and the various distribution intermediaries.

But unless Market Surveys are done appropriately, such that the data obtained are valid and accurate, their value is spurious. To be actionable, they must be representative of the universe of current and prospective users of the products, services or brands involved, and must be objectively obtained with samples large enough for measurement to be accurate.

Tracking Study

Tracking Studies are useful for determining brand awareness and purchase behavior. These are normally done to assess how things are going in the marketplace, but they certainly have value in developing marketing strategy as well. Tracking Studies, as the name implies, track an activity over a period of time. They can take the form of an ongoing survey of consumer usage, attitudes or buyer satisfaction. Tracking Studies are generally good at measuring results and explaining sales data. Better still, they include data that can be helpful in planning as well.

One good example of a Tracking Study is one which our firm conducted for the *Ryerson Company,* this country's biggest metal distributor. We were asked by the company to conduct a customer satisfaction research study of its clients to assess their attitudes toward *Ryerson* and its competition. The goal was to determine which companies provided the best customer satisfaction and why. I outlined this research study in detail in Lesson 3. Essentially, our test tracked the attitudes of customers over time and identified five factors which contributed to a customer's decision to work with a particular supplier. The five reasons became the hub of both *Ryerson's* marketing communications efforts and its key operational policies. I am pleased to report that implementing changes based on this research had a profound impact on customer satisfaction with *Ryerson* and on the company's financial business performance.

Concept Test

A *Concept Test* is a technique for determining consumer interest in a new product. Consumers are exposed to a number of product ideas in some form short of the actual physical product. The stimulus can be a descriptive paragraph on a card, a storyboard or a finished advertisement. In its most sophisticated form, an example of the product may be shown to the consumer. After exposure, the consumers are expected to make a choice among concepts. Their response is then analyzed and translated into a prediction of whether or not they would be interested in buying the product.

The fact that apples and oranges are often being compared seems to deter very few people from using this technique. That we expect consumers to fully comprehend what they are being asked to judge – and that they are dealing with a straw-man situation they are not apt to care about – does not seem to bother many researchers. However, the Concept Test can be useful at the earliest stages of new product development.

Package Test

A *Package Test* is employed to evaluate packages for both new and existing products. Package Tests are typically conducted directly with consumers either in person or online. Consumers are shown a package concept and asked if they like it and if they would consider buying the product. This is very preliminary research. It can be helpful in determining if a product has appeal for consumers and if it will stand out versus the competition. In my opinion, the Package Test cannot be viewed as a scientifically predictive tool. A more complex and reliable method of testing packages is in an on-shelf placement situation directly in the marketplace. This is explained under In-Store Testing below.

Copy Test

One doesn't need to do a basic market study every time one wants some consumer information. There are a number of instances when a Product Test or a Copy Test can yield all that is necessary for guiding strategy. We cannot be rigid about this matter. Our objective should always be to use whatever information we have as long as we can trust its accuracy and timeliness.

A ***Copy Test*** is a test to determine if one or several executions of an advertising campaign is effectively communicating the brand's positioning. While the test gets its name because the ad features ***Advertising Copy*** based on the advertising strategy, the copy is essentially being tested within an actual (sometimes roughly) produced commercial. One example of this type of test is an ***Audience Response Test*** where consumers are exposed to a series of advertisements, which includes the new ad being tested. The following day, the researchers follow up with the consumer to ask them which commercials they remember. This is the key outcome of the test – how many consumers "recall" the ad. The percent of recall for the ad being tested is compared to that of past ads – and also sometimes to other similar executions of the same brand's strategy.

While a simple Copy Test is useful for measuring if an advertisement is memorable, unfortunately, it does not measure the consumer's attitude toward the ad. It cannot necessarily predict whether the consumer liked the product concept and might be motivated to buy it based on the ad. A piece of advertising is not a product, and exposing it once is not a campaign. Thus, these tests do not provide a scientific determination of whether an ad will help translate into actual product sales. At best, this type of test will confirm that copy on the same strategy will yield similar results.

On the other hand, more sophisticated Copy Testing, which involves scientific methodology, can be extremely helpful in proving the effectiveness of advertising in communicating a brand's positioning or strategy. A good example of this is a research study which our firm conducted for *Procter & Gamble,* a major consumer products manufacturer.

Case Study: Jif Peanut Butter

In the 1970s, *Procter & Gamble* approached our firm to ask us to design a tailored Copy Test to determine if the advertising strategy being used for its large Jif Peanut Butter brand was most effectively addressing the consumer's motivation to purchase the product.

At that time, the product's target market was mothers with children, since we knew from our research that children were heavy users of peanut butter. The buying incentive being pitched to these mothers was that, because the product was easier to spread, easier to swallow and just a bit sweeter, it would please their children more than any other peanut butter brand. In other words, the advertising's message was "child-focused." This strategy was supported by historical copy testing.

A few years into this campaign strategy, sales of the brand were off – even after a long flight of TV advertising. Management asked our firm to look at the brand's advertising in terms of both message and execution. We proposed a sophisticated Copy Test. Instead of just asking people directly what they thought of the brand, we asked them to respond to a very large number of product qualities. We devised a special questioning board and cards. This permitted us to cover a much broader spectrum of possibilities, more than in the standard Copy Test. Then, with the use of some sophisticated new statistical techniques, we learned what product qualities were now most important to customers. We also learned which qualities had leverage – that is, which were most likely to move the consumer to purchase the brand.

So what did this high-powered tool tell us? To our surprise, the test revealed that the Jif consumer was not motivated by her child's preference of peanut butter, as management believed, but by her own perception of the quality of the product. It became clear that on the most critical point – **Buying Incentive** – our consumer preferred Jif over the competition because of several perceived product quality benefits. The idea of peanut taste and aroma was important. But more important was freshness – particularly as it related to their perception of its nutritional value. In other words, a combination of peanut taste, flavor and wholesomeness as demonstrated by the product's freshness appeared to be the critical lever.

As a result of this learning, the brand advertising was moved completely away from a "child-focused" message. The focal point now was the mother's opinion of the product's best qualities. In future campaigns, the advertising was based on this valuable information, derived from systematic and explicit copy testing. The new campaign increased Jif's share of the peanut butter category significantly.

Product Test

A ***Product Test*** can play an integral role in the development of new or repositioned products. Product tests can take many forms. The most common is the ***In-Home Test,*** where consumers are given a product and asked to try it for a few weeks. At the end of the period, they complete a survey or participate in an interview or Focus Group, where their attitudes toward the product and their interest in purchasing it can be quantitatively measured. While this test relies on subjective consumer input, it does have scientific merit because it is done with a large sample size and measures projectable results. These tests are especially helpful in the refinement of the profile and physical details of a product.

Product Tests are particularly important in the food industry, where taste is a key component of product acceptance. Often these tests can play a critical role in assessing the potential for a product's success in the marketplace. Unfortunately, there are many examples of misdirected and poorly designed research, occasionally with disastrous results for the brand.

Case Study: New Coke

A good example of a misguided Product Test is the *Coca-Cola Company's* introduction of New Coke in 1985. Sales of the company's flagship brand, known today as "Coca-Cola Classic," had been slipping. Preliminary research showed that some Coke users were switching to the sweeter-tasting Pepsi-Cola. Although I was not a party to what happened on the market research front, it is now apparent what mistakes were made.

Coca-Cola devoted serious R&D resources to the taste problem, developing a slightly sweeter product, which maintained its "Coke" integrity but was closer to the taste profile of Pepsi. The researchers ordered a traditional paired comparison test, pitting the New Coke against Pepsi in a blind situation, where consumers did not know which brand they were tasting. Overall, New Coke was preferred. The company then replaced the old formula with the new one, developed a new package and put enormous financial resources behind the new product. They positioned it as a new and improved version of their beloved brand, only to see it flop in the marketplace. Consumers wanted their Coke back, which is what the company promptly and wisely gave them.

What is clear in hindsight was that the researchers failed to understand the marketing issues at stake. If they were really au courant with the marketing process, they would have insisted on first conducting a discrimination test with each consumer in the study and then implementing a paired comparison with those who could tell the difference in taste between one brand and the other. Had that been done, I am sure they would have learned that a majority of cola consumers either could not tell the difference or preferred a sweeter Pepsi-like taste. But they also would have learned that a substantial number of cola drinkers could tell the difference between the two brands and that a sizable number, albeit not a majority, liked the original Coca-Cola formulation. Under such circumstances, the researchers could easily have recommended introducing the new Coke as a line extension instead of taking the old formula off the market. Fortunately for *Coca-Cola*, its management was flexible enough to correct the error early in the game.

The failure of New Coke was not a lack of technique, a lack of data or the unwillingness of management to do market research. Instead it was a failure in research design, a failure that didn't help the image of market research one bit. Ironically, the subsequent reintroduction of Coke's original formula, re-branded as "Coca-Cola Classic," resulted in a significant gain in sales. The new Coke, which was renamed "Coke 2" and positioned as "the new taste of Coca-Cola," is no longer in distribution.

Market Testing: An Overview

Test Marketing is one of those primary research concepts with a number of names. Some call it *Market Testing,* others call it *In-Market Testing,* and still others call it *Pilot Testing. Market Testing,* as I prefer to call it, is a simple attempt to use the actual marketplace experimentally. It is a controlled experiment, done in a limited but carefully related area of the marketplace, whose aim is to predict the sales or profit consequences, either in absolute or relative terms, of one or more proposed marketing actions. Companies often use these tests when they are considering a marketing activity which will require a major financial investment.

In more specific scientific terms, Market Testing's predictive use is to evaluate alternative individual marketing variables. Here we are not concerned with measuring the effect of the total marketing mix, but rather with a single variable of that mix or, as is often the case, one variable versus another, usually the one in use. For example, Market Tests are often used to determine the extent to which a new media pattern is better than an existing one, or one distribution method is more effective than another, or a higher advertising budget is more profitable than a lower one. Any subdivisions of these variables are also susceptible to test. One might choose to learn whether nighttime television expenditures produce more sales than the same expenditures in daytime television.

Before we move on to the specifics of Market Testing, I'd like to take a moment to offer some philosophical thoughts. To the research-oriented person, the term *Market Test* has a precise meaning. To him it is a controlled experiment, done in a limited but carefully selected part of the marketplace, whose aim is to predict the sales or profit consequences, either in absolute or relative terms, of one or more proposed marketing actions. It is the use of the marketplace as a laboratory, as well as the use of direct sales measurement, which differentiate this test from other types of market research. The **Checkerboard Test** which I will describe at the end of this Lesson can be used to ascertain which of a number of marketing variables is more effective when used in the marketplace. Certainly, you will see that the work my firm did for *H&R Block* was used successfully for this purpose.

At the other extreme, Market Testing has the very loose meaning of merely "trying something out" in the marketplace. This meaning is commonly held by, although hardly limited to, the self-made businessman. A substantial number of entrepreneurs have established successful businesses built to a large extent on this process of trying something out. The proprietors of these businesses often had an idea, pragmatically tried it out in a market or two, succeeded, and went on to succeed on a larger scale, either regionally or nationally. Needless to say, those who followed this simple approach on a small scale but failed when they went national are not pushing it very hard. We therefore do not hear much about the unsuccessful side of this approach. Like stock market investors, we hear only from the winners.

Of course, between the two extremes of scientific testing and trying something out, there is room for many different degrees of experimentation. Often the choice of a Market Test design between these two extremes is governed by the budget. While Market Testing may be both a useful and a desirable managerial-control tool, in my experience, its results are more scientifically predictive if management chooses the right test and puts adequate resources behind it.

Types of Market Testing

Market Testing is most often used as a predictive device in two situations: the introduction of a new product and the repositioning of an existing brand. I would like to share four popular methods for Market Testing which are used for both situations with varying degrees of quantifiable results. They are: 1) the In-Store Test, 2) the Single Market Test, 3) the Mini-Market Test, and 4) the Checkerboard Test.

In-Store Test

The *In-Store Test* is a small-scale controlled test which is most commonly used to evaluate a change in one marketing variable for an established brand. For example, an In-Store Test can be used to determine if a revised package or a new price will affect a brand's sales and profitability.

When this test is done well, the stores within a market are usually randomly split into two groups. To use the packaging example, one package is put into one group of stores and a second package is put into a second group. To prevent extraneous differences between the two groups from distorting the test, the variables should be crossed over every month. This activity must be carefully controlled.

Most of the time, In-Store Tests are conducted in one market or, at most, in a few markets. The assumption is that the between-city variation is less than the within-city variation. If so, the test may yield a decisive result, particularly when properly handled. These tests have been used effectively for checking whether a variable that does not need advertising or promotion (some action outside the store) is uneconomic. If In-Store Tests were done in a number of places and if similar results were obtained, even if the results were not perfectly projectable, a marketer could feel more secure in moving forward with a change on a larger scale. But because its value is only where an in-store variable is testable, this test's usefulness is limited.

Single Market Test

The *Single Market Test* is the introduction of a product into a specific market as a way of previewing how it will perform in the marketplace. It has value as a learning tool for both new products and for me-too products being introduced into a new market or region for the first time. The Single Market Test can be extremely useful as a training device. It can help companies discover problems that can be found only when the product is actually in the marketplace. For example, a single market test might be used to test a new formulation of a product such as *Kleenex*, where the box might collapse on the shelf because a modified package reacted to dampness in the store.

It is best to think about the Single Market Test as a trial run because it is generally not quantitatively-based and therefore will not be predictive of sales in any meaningful or projectable way. Nevertheless, much can be learned just from placing a product into distribution and seeing what happens in the real marketplace.

Mini-Market Test

The third form of Market Testing we will discuss is the *Mini-Market Test,* which is conducted under very unique market conditions. Like the Single Market Test, this method attempts to replicate real market conditions in order to measure the validity of marketing variables. It is especially popular for new product introductions.

Companies like *Behaviorscan* developed the Mini-Market concept in the 1980s. Essentially, the test involves introducing a product into one or two markets – Pittsfield, Massachusetts and Grand Junction, Colorado are examples – which have been established as actual test settings. Because the research company is able to assert control over key marketing variables, such as price, distribution and advertising, these factors can be monitored throughout the test and later evaluated. Benefits of the Mini-Market Test include the test market's sophisticated infrastructure, the substantial amount and kinds of data which it generates, and the speed with which results can be obtained.

In my view, however, while many marketplace variables are carefully measured in the Mini-Market Test, it is difficult to see how it can accurately project to the greater marketplace. There are too many controlled variables which are virtually impossible to replicate. For example, the product gets 100% in-store distribution, atypical media are used to reach the market and a large percentage of people in the town are sampled. While there is no doubt excellent learning to be mined from the myriad reports generated, as well as the actual in-market presence of the product, the methodological requirements are just not in place to make this test truly predictive or translatable into business results in the broader marketplace.

Author's Contribution: The creation of a novel, systematic approach to testing market variables

The Checkerboard Test

The final market testing technique we will examine, the **Checkerboard Test**, is designed to reliably predict the impact of a single or multiple marketing variables in the marketplace.

Case Study: The H&R Block Company

In 1975, my consulting firm had the privilege of developing an extensive market testing methodology for the *H&R Block Company*, "The Income Tax People," as they called themselves then. This totally novel approach to market testing cast new light on the use of the marketplace as a means for evaluating the effectiveness of marketing variables in a quantifiable and scientifically-valid way.

Developed over a 10-year partnership between *H&R Block* and our firm, the Checkerboard Test represented a revolutionary approach to testing multiple marketing variables. The concept is modeled after the way that farmers plant their crops in a checkerboard formation – on square fields next to but separated from one another – so that they can determine which crop will yield the best output. Similarly, the Checkerboard Test design divides the marketplace into unique retail squares and, by placing different marketing variables next to one another, reveals the relative effectiveness of each. The beauty of the test we developed for *H&R Block* was that the squares, in this case, "blocks" consisting of stores providing retail tax preparation services, constituted a representative sample which could accurately predict which variables would be most effective when replicated in the national marketplace.

As you'll see from my description of our firm's longitudinal research project, the Checkerboard model represented a new and important application of quantitative testing to the field of market research. The best indicator of its success at the time was that, after the company integrated our findings into its **Strategic Marketing Planning Process,** it consistently showed significantly improved business performance.

Test design and Unique Features

Our firm was hired by *H&R Block's* founder, Henry Block, to help the company better understand how its different marketing variables – including media spending levels, pricing and copy executions – were working in the marketplace. After a very preliminary review of the business, it became clear to us that, because of its in-depth national presence, the company was ideally suited to targeted experimentation in the marketplace.

We got to work designing an extensive, relatively inexpensive in-market Checkerboard Test. These were the market conditions which made this design possible:

1) The company owned more than 5000 retail offices, covering over 75% of the United States.

2) The company used only local media – newspapers and spot broadcasts. Moreover, it planned and bought its own media so it could control exactly what it did in each market.

3) The company's service – the preparation of income tax forms – is used by just about every household in the U.S. Moreover, the service is bought locally. No wholesalers

are involved and the product is produced and sold in the local area. Further, the product is bought only once a year during the first four months, so there is no seasonality.

4) The company maintained a complete computerized data file of its sales and other critical market information. As a consequence, a census of unit and dollar sales could be obtained for any time period necessary at very little cost.

5) Finally, the company had no major national competition. While the actions of any individual competitor could affect *H&R Block's* sales in a particular market, none could influence it in the total country.

Specific assumptions

1) Armed with these fortuitous market conditions, we developed a set of assumptions to facilitate the development of the Checkerboard Test design. Our assumptions stipulated that:

2) Television markets, as defined by the *Advertising Research Bureau,* are mutually exclusive media/market areas.

3) The **Areas of Dominant Influence** (ADIs) can be randomly divided into relatively large experimental groups of noncontiguous markets, each of which is no less than 15% of the total marketing universe involved.

4) A single marketing variable is injected into one or more of the experimental test groups. If enough groups exist, one or more groups can be used as a control, depending on what the test is trying to measure.

5) Unit and dollar sales are measured at each local retail outlet within each ADI and summed into its experimental group. In essence, a census of sales is obtained.

Advantage over traditional in-market tests

The beauty of the national Checkerboard Test design is that it eliminates the three major shortcomings of traditional in-Market Test methods.

First, in traditional tests, either a few small markets are used or a large, relatively homogeneous region is selected. Often a control group is matched, conceivably to make the markets comparable. Unfortunately, they always remain unrepresentative of the universe. This is not the case with the national Checkerboard Test. There is no problem of market experimental groups; all are large – somewhere between 16% and 33% of the universe. The ADIs are all chosen randomly, so that each ADI is given an equal chance of inclusion in each group. Thus, each experimental group is a representation of the total to be measured. The entire trading universe is involved in the test. The ADIs are a very diverse group, consisting of different sizes and profiles, and are geographically dispersed at random.

Second, in traditional market tests, there is a problem of controlling the variables – of isolating the item being measured from so-called extraneous forces. This is circumvented in the national Checkerboard Test design in two ways. Everything is locally controlled. All media are bought in the local area. All prices and promotional activities are locally determined. Moreover, so many different markets are used in each experimental group (minimally about 25) that the ability of most extraneous variables to affect the total is eliminated. While an unanticipated local event could affect a single ADI, its influence can hardly affect the total result.

And finally, in traditional market tests, the problems of measurement are especially difficult – of getting enough outlets in the sample, of measuring units, of properly acquiring inventories and of covering all types of outlets, to mention the most critical ones. Not so with the national Checkerboard Test design. Unit sales were measured in every outlet at the retail level. No wholesalers were involved, so there were no transfer shipments. No inventories were involved, no repeat sales, no seasonality. Everything was neat and clean.

Findings for Different Marketing Variables

Over the course of a decade, the Checkerboard Test proved a fascinating and extremely effective method by which to test the impact of an array of marketing variables in quantifiable market situations. In our discussion of strategic marketing planning in Lesson 3, I pointed out the importance of conducting ongoing market research even as plans are being implemented in the marketplace. There is no better example of following this directive than *H&R Block,* which continuously questioned assumptions about marketing variables, tested different options in the marketplace, and used that research both for future planning and to modify its business activities on an ongoing basis. I am pleased to highlight a few examples of this below.

Evaluating alternative campaigns

Our first learning was in testing alternative advertising campaigns. The company assumed that some executions were more effective than others in communicating a brand positioning or strategy. They likewise assumed that such differences would translate into sales.

Over a five-year period, *H&R Block* had been running two different advertising campaigns based on the same strategy in the marketplace. The proportion of the country used for each depended on how well each commercial did in copy pretests or in the marketplace the previous year. What we found was that when we tested different campaigns against one another in the marketplace, the differences were never very large. For example, one campaign generated 1-2% more revenue than the other. However, from management's point of view, a 2% or 3% increase in unit sales added up to a lot of profit dollars. Hence, the tests were useful in identifying the economic value of different advertising executions.

Impact of price increases

The company had been raising its prices each year, often more than the inflation rate, and kept increasing its profits substantially. But Henry Block was concerned that the price increases kept the company from growing units, i.e., increasing its number of consumers. We launched an intensive in-market test of price elasticity, followed by an in-depth statistical analysis of the company's sales data. Both studies affirmed that Block's concerns were valid and that the company should not raise its prices by more than the previous year's inflation rate.

Block then asked our firm to confirm this by conducting a follow-up test in the marketplace. We divided the country into two parts: in one, the company raised the price somewhat above inflation, and in the other, the inflation rate was used. We found that sticking to the lower price increased unit sales substantially over the higher-priced markets – and thus it was the better strategy. It is my understanding that *H&R Block* followed that strategy until Henry Block retired.

Comparison of new vs. old campaign

Another issue we were able to explore in the Checkerboard Test design was advertising campaign wear-out. *H&R Block* had been running two television campaigns for a number of years. Although marketplace results indicated that the campaigns had probably run their course, the agency was reluctant to give them up. It was therefore decided to vary the budget on both a new campaign and the old campaign to see if it would make a difference in unit sales. Since there was some skepticism on the company's part that the old campaign would perform, it was placed in only one-third of the country.

What we learned from the marketplace was that increasing the budget on the old campaign yielded a slightly negative result. Decreasing the budget added 1.9% to unit sales. The difference between the higher and lower budget was 2.1%. On the other hand, raising the budget on the new campaign had a very positive effect, while lowering it had a negative effect on sales. The research provided quantitative proof that it was time to move on to the new campaign.

Effectiveness of advertising copy

Finally, the Checkerboard Test method proved an excellent vehicle for evaluating the impact of the variable of advertising copy on the product's marketing plan. This was apparent when we tested two different advertising campaigns. The strategy for the campaigns was the same, but they were differently executed. Thus, the campaign copy was the key independent variable.

Over the period of a year, we tested the campaign in 25 different ADIs. Within the two experimental groups, 75% got campaign A and 25% got campaign B. We viewed the change in unit sales for the two experimental groups. We found that the variation in the larger part was 25.0% – ranging from +1.6% to -24.0%. In the smaller part, the variation was 16.9% – ranging from +0.8% to -16.1%. This turned out to be the case over several years.

What these results said very clearly, when compared with the different campaign results, is that there is far more variation within test groups than across them. This could only be the result of other variables playing a far bigger role in unit sales than the variable we were testing – copy. It also explains why traditional market tests of individual marketing variables conducted in a few markets rarely obtain conclusive results. Further, it explains why market tests of new market entries, which involve a number of variables combined together, have a greater validity than those testing single variables. Once again, the importance of isolating variables so that they can be evaluated via reliable quantitative analysis is clear.

Broader Implications of the Checkerboard Test

My 10-year project with *H&R Block* was certainly a highpoint of my career. Our firm's ability to use the resources of this well-established, well-endowed company led to the creation of a novel, more scientifically-valid approach to testing individual market variables. Of course, not all companies are as ideally set up as *Block* was – with broad national distribution, multiple communications options and easily definable market "blocks." Nevertheless, the Checkerboard model proved extremely effective at accurately assessing individual marketing variables in the marketplace and has broad potential for use in our increasingly global economy. With the continued ascendancy of so-called Superstores and the expansion of powerful national chains – especially those which collect their own national sales data – the potential for using this methodology by companies like *Home Depot, Costco, McDonald's* and *Target* is obvious.

Conclusion

In summary, I hope that I have effectively communicated in this Lesson the value of applying scientific research to marketing planning. My message is really a simple one. Only well-crafted quantitative research methods will help management achieve its overall goals of identifying opportunities and reducing business risk.

There is no abracadabra or divining rod in market research. If there is any magic involved at all, it is the magic that comes from disciplined management, and the use and implementation of research – from sticking with the basics and avoiding the quick and dirty techniques that serve only to confuse the key issues.

True, companies may have to restrict the number of business opportunities they can invest in or new products they can develop to afford this disciplined approach. In so doing, they may occasionally miss a winner. But, as in poker, the winners usually play fewer hands. They go out when their hands are poor. They stay in to exploit the good ones. Only losers rely on magic.

In our next Lesson, we will take our research discussion one step further, for an in-depth look at how to measure whether advertising is effectively reaching the right audience the right number of times.

Lesson 5:

Identifying real media exposure is critical to evaluating advertising effectiveness

"The medium is the message."

*– Social Critic Marshall McLuhan
on the growing power of commercial television*

It's probably hard for you to imagine a time when television was not a vital part of American culture. But when Marshall McLuhan crafted these immortal words in 1964, TV had been a mainstay in the majority of American households for less than a decade. McLuhan's bold assertion, part of a landmark study called "Understanding Media," posited that the form of a medium embeds itself in the message, creating a symbiotic relationship by which the medium influences how the message is perceived. In other words, the way a message is delivered is as important as the message itself.

I'm sure you'll see how this idea can easily be applied to the practice of marketing and, in particular, advertising. As we've seen in our discussions of **Strategic Marketing Planning,** to be successful in selling a brand, an advertisement must soundly execute the brand's marketing strategy. But how that execution is delivered – which medium is used and how it is used – is also an integral part of ensuring that sale. So, while the message of an ad is important, if it doesn't have effective exposure, it won't be successful in persuading the consumer and ultimately generating sales.

But, before we get deeper into the discussion of how to evaluate advertising's effectiveness, I'd like to share some ideas I've developed over the years about how agencies and their clients can work together to create great advertising.

The Role of Advertising

In my six decades of experience, it has become clear to me that the most important marketing variable in determining business success is brand communications or advertising. Simply put, advertising has two very specific roles. The first is to convey information about the qualities and benefits of a product, thereby identifying its brand name and what it stands for. The second role of advertising is to persuade prospective buyers to choose one brand instead of a competitor in its product category. Advertising that fails to persuade the prospective buyers to respond in some way has failed in its role. It is therefore the aim of the seller to create advertising and place it in the media so it can generate a strong enough positive attitude toward a brand that the prospective customer will be motivated to purchase it.

As we can deduce from Mr. McLuhan's assertion, advertising has two components: 1) *The Message* (what the advertising consists of) and 2) *The Medium* (how one puts resources against that message to reach the target consumer). Let's look at these in more specific terms.

What is the message?

The *Message* of an advertisement should be compelling and persuasive, and should reflect the brand's marketing strategy. A good use of consumer research, combined with well-articulated direction from the client and concurrence from the agency, should produce the desired execution. In the end, if a strategically-sound campaign effectively reaches a target consumer, its message should impact consumer behavior. It should both shift attitudes and persuade consumers to buy the product.

What is the medium?

The *Medium* is essentially the way that the message is delivered. It can be national or regional, in television or print, online or on billboards. Within each of these media, there are additional options: cable shows or newspapers, youtube or subway stations. The bottom line is that choosing the right medium will impact how well the message reaches the consumer and, ultimately, how well the product will perform.

Everyone knows that the message is important. If you develop a solid brand strategy, you can develop great advertising which effectively communicates it. But we've now established that the next step, the media selected, is also important to success.

Guidelines for Successful Brand Communications

In Lesson 6, I will talk in detail about how a symbiotic relationship between the client and its agency will lead to the creation of an on-target message and the optimum media mix. At this juncture, however, I would like to offer some guidelines I have gained over six decades about what generates the best brand communications.

Carefully define the strategy

The basic advertising strategy, not the execution, is what makes advertising effective. A great execution can enhance the effectiveness of a well-grounded strategy. However, no execution, regardless of how "creative," can of itself result in effective advertising if it is not strategically driven.

Combine research and judgement

A marketer must give the agency the right tools. An ad campaign must be based on a combination of systematic and explicit analysis, as well as a considerable amount of thoughtful and experienced judgement. It must rest on a sound strategic foundation – not on the whims, guesses or intuitions of creative people or, for that matter, clients.

Build brand awareness

For an agency to produce effective advertising, it must focus on the goal – which is to build, strengthen and enhance brand awareness and the reputation of what is being offered. Consumer behavior must ultimately manifest itself in sales, but these sales are the result of everything a company does, not merely its marketing communications. What a company must seek is profitable sales, because profitability is what allows a company to survive and prosper. And increased profitability is what building sustainable brands is all about.

Think long-term

Brand communications should reflect long-term thinking. We are not sales-driven; we should not create ads for the sole sake of making immediate sales. We are brand-driven; we create advertising and other marketing communications so that a brand will be perceived as desirable, valuable and worthy of purchase over the long-term.

The ultimate aim of brand communications is to help generate incremental revenue for the brand and to differentiate it in a meaningful way from its competition. Advertising by itself cannot consummate a transaction. It can, at best, only lead to one.

Theodore Levitt explained the value of communications more eloquently when he wrote:

> "Neither the poet nor the adman celebrates the literal functionality of what he produces. Instead, each celebrates a deep and complex emotion which he symbolizes by creative embellishment – a content which cannot be captured by literal description alone. Communication through advertising or through poetry or through any other medium is a

creative conceptualization that implies a vicarious experience through a language of symbolic substitutes.

Communication can never be the real thing it talks about. Therefore, all communication is in some inevitable fashion a departure from reality. No one lives by facts alone. We all need to know why as well as what. Consumers buy goods and services to satisfy their needs and wants. When advertising indicates how a product's attribute will satisfy a need or want, it's being persuasive. If it conveys this persuasive information honestly and openly, no manipulation is involved.

–Theodore Levitt, Marketing Scholar

To paraphrase the legendary Dr. Levitt, no one lives by facts alone. We all need to know why as well as what. So, while a well-crafted, strategically-based message is critical, that message must be intimately joined with the right medium in order to be truly persuasive.

The Role of Media Planning

No matter how brilliant the creative message or execution of an advertisement is, without proper media placement, a TV commercial is just an in-house movie, and a print ad is just a pretty picture on the wall. Media are the means of delivering the advertising message. Unless the placement is done properly, nothing will happen in the marketplace.

Media planning and buying are among the most complicated aspects of advertising. In the last few decades, the role and function of media planning has become more complex – and more critical. That's because, over time, almost every national advertiser of any size has spent more and more of its advertising money on television. It was obvious to me, beginning in 1955, that that the major media issues were not about what media to use, but rather how to use and buy television as efficiently as possible. This, with the possible of exception of the burgeoning online media business, is still true today.

Reach and Frequency:
Building blocks of media planning

To help direct our discussion about evaluating the effectiveness of media, let's take a step back and consider why two terms which are considered the most essential elements of a media plan – **Reach and Frequency** – are so important. An advertiser rarely buys just a single ad or commercial. Media audiences duplicate each other. That is, people don't isolate their media exposure to a single TV show, radio station, website or magazine. They're exposed to multiple media. The advertiser needs to know how many different people its schedule will reach and how many times (meaning, with what frequency) its schedule will be exposed to them.

You might wonder: Don't all media combinations tend to reach about the same number of different people as long as they stay within the same general ballpark and deliver about the same number of rating points?

Not necessarily. Let's use home construction as an analogy. Say you have twelve bricks and you want to build a house. You have many options. To name just two, you can build a narrow six-story house by stacking two columns of six bricks. Or you can build a low, wide ranch house by stacking four columns of three bricks. In the same way you can take a given number of media rating points (or bricks) and build either a high-reaching structure with limited foot frontage (meaning reach) or a limited-reaching structure with broad foot frontage (meaning frequency).

Just as a homebuilder uses different plans to construct different homes, a media strategist uses different plans to build different media structures. And just as the number of stories of a building times its base gives you the gross area or square footage, so the reach of a media plan times the frequency gives you what's known in the business as GRPs.

Evaluating a media plan

When television became the primary source of media delivery, the key analytical tool was a measurement called **Gross Rating Points** or **GRPs.** A **GRP** is equal to the percent or number of households (not people) who have the opportunity to be exposed to a commercial at a particular time. This exposure results when the television set is tuned into to a specific channel or program. Thus, a program rating of 20 means that 20% of all turned-on sets in the country are tuned in to a particular program. It says nothing about anyone watching or listening to the set – either the program or the commercials.

Let's look a bit more closely at how a media plan's effectiveness was historically determined. From the onset, GRPs were used to measure the total exposure opportunities for an advertisement. For example, an advertiser who buys 400 GRPs during a particular time period presumably will reach 80% of all households an average of five times. But this doesn't mean every household is exposed to the commercial five times. On the contrary: a number of different **Reach and Frequency** combinations will produce the same 400 GRP results. One could obtain 400 GRPs with a 57% reach and an average frequency of 7; or with a 67% reach and frequency of 6; or with a reach of 89% and frequency of 4.5. In each case, the total exposure is the same, yet we have three rather different situations.

In the early 1970s, it became clear to me that using GRPs to evaluate a media plan had two fatal flaws: 1) GRPs measure only *opportunities* for exposure to an advertisement – not actual exposures, and 2) Many people who get exposed do not get enough exposure to do something about it. That is, the GRPs don't take into account the known fact that many people who have the TV, radio or computer turned on don't watch or listen to the commercials, and don't watch them enough to form an opinion about what they have seen or heard. This is especially relevant today when much of television programming is watched via DVRs, streaming and even binge viewing. The same holds true for print media – many people don't look at the ads in magazines or online, and many who have seen them once won't look at them again.

Author's Contribution: The development of the effective rating point tool to improve the assessment of advertising effectiveness

I believe that one of my most important contributions to the Advertising industry was the development of **Effective Exposure** as an assessment tool. I would like now to explain to you how using this method to develop a media plan (versus the traditional GRPs) will provide a much better assessment of **Reach and Frequency** for an ad – and will deliver results in the marketplace.

In the late 1970s, in an effort to make advertising analysis more accurate, I created the concept of *Effective Exposure* and its measuring stick, *Effective Rating Points* or ERPs. My concept was based on the idea that it takes a certain number of actual exposures to an advertisement before it has an impact on the viewer or reader. In other words, a person must see and/or hear a television advertisement a certain number of times before he or she can absorb it and consider acting on it. In contrast, GRPs are based on the idea that all exposures are equal and have an equal effect. As we've established, however, the reality of consumer's fickle TV viewership behavior demands that some adjustment be made for the differential effect.

The Effective Exposure Theory

I based my *Effective Exposure Theory* on six studies conducted between 1963 and 1972 by corporations, universities and research institutions. The studies, each of which built loosely on the prior study's learning, revealed several fundamental facts about the realities of TV advertising viewership. The research showed that:

- As a person is exposed to verbal or visual stimuli, his or her response or learning increases until it reaches a point of wear-out or satiation – and then starts to decline.

- The satiation point for learning from an advertisement peaks at between three and five exposures. Additional exposures are followed by a decline in information gain.

- The optimum number of exposures for an advertisement to impact brand attitudes is about 10. After this point, negative consumer reaction surpasses positive brand attitudes.

- And finally, the minimum number of exposures to an advertisement needed for impact is three. The first exposure addresses the viewer's question: "What is it?" The second exposure answers: "What of it?" And the third exposure is the reminder that mixes the answers of the two questions and jells them in the viewer's mind. Psychologically, there's no such thing as a fourth exposure. Rather, the fourth exposure is merely repetition number one of the third. The third exposure also marks the beginning of disengagement, as the viewer withdraws attention because there are no more questions to be answered.

Implications for measuring advertising effectiveness

These studies led me to draw the following conclusions: 1) The first two exposures to a television advertisement have little value. Individuals with fewer than three exposures aren't significantly affected by the ad. 2) Little further benefit comes from more than ten exposures to an ad within a given time period. 3) More than fifteen exposures to an ad can have a negative effect.

Thus I inferred that, optimally, a target audience should be exposed to an advertisement between three and ten times. It is important to keep in mind that Effective Exposure is based on the fact that not every exposure is of equal value. If all exposures had equal value, only one exposure would be needed to make a sale. Why bother with *Frequency* if only *Reach* is necessary?

There's a good deal of logic in applying the law of diminishing returns to advertising effectiveness. It seems quite intuitive that, after a number of exposures to an ad, very little more can be learned from additional exposures, and the ability to persuade diminishes thereafter. But if we accept this evidence and the logic behind it, we must accept its corollary: that only part of the *Exposure Frequency Distribution* resulting from an advertising campaign is effective – the part between three and ten exposures.

We might say that the reach obtained before the third exposure is ineffective exposure; that after the tenth, it is excessive exposure; and that after the fifteenth exposure it can be considered negative exposure. But it's important to note that the eleventh through fifteenth exposures aren't all waste; they are just redundant. The first ten exposures have value. It's just after the tenth that viewing the ad becomes superfluous.

Think back to the example I gave earlier, of an advertiser who buys 400 GRPs during a particular time period. Using my concept of Effective Exposure, the ERPs obtained would be 221, as opposed to the 400 GRPs obtained using the concept of total exposure. In other words, in this example, just over half the advertising purchased would be effective—that is, the ad would be seen frequently enough to have an effect.

Challenges for media planning

The Effective Exposure Theory has enormous implications, not only in terms of how advertisers value their media buys in general, but also in terms of the media mix and advertising budgets. Of course, the potential pitfall with Effective Exposure is that, by accurately determining how many exposures actually occur, it corrects only one of the flaws in GRPs. The other is that, nowadays, not very many people who have the opportunity to be exposed to advertisements take the opportunity to watch them.

The problem is that advertising's ubiquity has alienated viewers of programming to the point where they take an active role with their computers and DVRs to eliminate as many of the ads as they can. This is compounded by the increased use of live streaming, which eliminates advertising from the mix completely. For reasons I do not understand, advertisers keep ignoring this issue. Going forward, media planners should make adjustments to take into consideration this concept of real exposure.

Conclusion

I fear that, in pointing out limitations in both GRPs and ERPs, I may have discouraged some potential advertisers from agreeing to any media plan at all. I want to emphasize one final time that the concept of ERPs as I defined it is an excellent and scientifically-valid means of assessing advertising effectiveness. If a media plan is crafted to deliver ERPs for a brand – and takes into consideration the novel means by which consumers view programming today – a strategically sound and engaging campaign is likely to deliver success in the marketplace.

This seems like a very appropriate time to move on to our final Lesson, which will explore in detail how relationships between advertisers and their agencies can be maximized.

Lesson 6:

A successful client-agency partnership will drive business and brand performance

"The relationship between a manufacturer and his agency is almost as intimate as the relationship between a patient and his doctor. Make sure that you can live happily with your prospective client before you accept the account."

—David Olgivy, The Father of Modern Advertising

Over the course of these Lessons, we have seen the process by which a brand's concept is established, its strategic plan is developed, its unique consumer benefits are vetted through scientifically-based research and, finally, the efficiency of its advertising is evaluated. In this sixth and final Lesson, we will focus on the final step in selling a product in the marketplace: The implementation of an **Effective Communications Strategy**. Specifically, we will see how the relationship between a marketer and its agency is a critical driver of business success in the marketplace.

More than any other aspect of the marketing mix, great brand communications depends on an effective partnership between a client and its agency. To realize brand success, the client-agency team must have a solid agreement on strategic goals, resource needs and business and service expectations. There must be mutual trust and respect between the partners, as well as a clear understanding of the agency's compensation structure.

Over the years, our firm made two important (and at the time revolutionary) contributions to the process of effectively matching agency and client needs to achieve business results. First, we established a formal **Competititve Agency Search Process** for helping clients select a communications agency which would best meet their needs. Second, we developed a systematic approach for helping marketers negotiate an equitable **Tailored Compensation Agreement** with their agency. I call these ideas revolutionary because, while today they are accepted standards in the industry, in the late 1970s, they were controversial.

But before I outline the specifics of the two systems we created, I would like to share some guidelines I developed over the years about how to achieve the most effective and mutually beneficial client-agency relationship. These Guidelines are based on countless lessons learned from my experience on both sides of the table: 1) as an advertising executive trying to represent my agency's strengths to a potential client in the best possible light, and 2) as a consultant trying to identify the ideal strategic agency partner for my client.

In total, our firm conducted 50 agency searches and negotiated 200 agency compensation agreements over more than three decades. Our clients included *Nissan, Hallmark, Minolta, Honda, General Foods, Chrysler, Hyundai, Western Union, Unisys* and many others – some more than once. In the process, I was exposed to detailed presentations and solicitations by more than 60 advertising, public relations and sales promotion agencies. The experience reinforced what should be intuitive: matching the needs of the client with the skills of the agency is the best predictor of business success.

Guidelines for Effective Client-Agency Partnerships

In these challenging times, one of the most valuable marketing tools may well be a strong sense of pragmatism. If we are to make advertising work harder, if we are to rejuvenate our marketing mechanism, we must examine the process as a whole and be willing to initiate change, wherever appropriate, to adapt to the external environment. Because objective measures of advertising productivity can sometimes prove elusive and expensive, the most intelligent thing we can do to maximize our potential for success is to make sure the institution responsible for the advertising – the communications agency – works collaboratively with the client in optimizing its output.

The most efficient and effective environment for marketing activities is a nurturing and mutually collaborative one. Gaining control of the media and producing advertising that sells is more likely to result from a solid client-agency relationship than from a single creative individual. Some fundamental Guidelines, expressed here from the client's perspective, maximize the chance for mutual client and agency success.

Communicate overall expectations

Make sure that you tell the agency, in writing, precisely what resources and services you expect from it. Discourage your agency from providing services you do not want without your prior approval. That will save you the resentment of paying for something you don't want or need. Likewise, nothing is more destructive to agency productivity than "make-work."

Agree on roles

Agree on exactly which aspects of the planning and communications process you and the agency will each be held responsible and accountable for. Concentrate on agency product, not process – you have your own business to run – and make sure that everyone in your organization adheres to that plan. Agree with your agency about the scope of its job, and then restrain yourself from doing its job. It is one thing for you to give broad direction, but quite another for you to write copy or specify media vehicles.

Eliminate agency compensation as an issue

If you are unhappy with your current arrangement, negotiate a new one that is mutually beneficial. Agree on exactly which services you are willing to pay for and which you are not. Make sure you allow the agency to make a fair, steady profit on a fee schedule that ensures you will pay only for what you get. Offer your agency an incentive: the better the relationship, the higher the fee. And whatever you do, put it in writing.

Communicate resource expectations

Emphasize to agency management your desire for a balanced team of people on your account, one that communicates with each other and with you. Good advertising never comes from just creative, account, media or research people. It comes from collaboration among them. One way to achieve such teamwork is by insisting that media people present media, research people present research and creative people present copy. This will ensure that every agency group is involved in your business and knows what is going on.

Insist on a strong account team

Make sure agency management knows that you expect to have a first-rate account team on the business and that it, not the creative group, is the focal point of the relationship. A client must have full confidence in the knowledge, intelligence, commitment and diligence of the account team. Expect team members to get out to the marketplace, visit stores, talk to the sales force and see facilities. Work through the account group. Nothing creates more confusion and reduced productivity than dealing with functional groups without the knowledge of the account team. Refuse to work with "yes-men." Enthusiasm and optimism are important, but realism is critical.

Share what you know

Recognize that market information is a crucial ingredient for effective advertising. Share whatever information you have with your agency, and make sure it shares with you. The more your agency knows about your business, the better the decisions it will make. Stupid mistakes usually stem from ignorance. Share your marketing plans, product information and finances with your agency. Insist, however, that the agency keep all information confidential and secure.

Agree on terminology

Misdirection comes from miscommunication. Definitions of important terms should be precise and put in writing. Otherwise, strategies will sound like tactics, and objectives may be construed as strategies.

Agree on an advertising plan

Have your agency prepare a written advertising plan or platform prior to the creation of advertising. Make sure it is consistent with your **Strategic Marketing Plan.** Insist on total marketing thinking, and encourage the agency to consider the entire communications mix. The more complete the communications plan, the more you can maintain accountability a year later. Require that the plan specifically addresses at least four important strategic elements in detail: 1) A clearly defined market target, 2) An expected source of business (competitors, market, segments or brands), 3) A distinctive and compelling selling proposition that can create a substantial competitive advantage with your market target, and 4) A media strategy that will optimize your exposure to the market target.

Develop a dialogue with top agency management

No one can solve festering problems better and faster than the people at the top. Without agreement and compatibility at the top, there is no agreement or compatibility anywhere in the relationship. Make sure that someone in the agency's top management takes personal responsibility for your business and for communicating decisions downward. Remember that most of the people who work on your account come and go. Top management is generally there for the duration. Avoid too many approval layers in your organization. Smart, experienced agency people expect to be treated with respect, and they have trouble dealing with a deep hierarchical approval structure at the client.

Cultivate a cordial, businesslike relationship

Agency people want to identify with you; treat them like collaborators, not suppliers or vendors. If you are unhappy about something or someone, don't delay your criticism. You would want similar treatment. Conflicts in opinion are good if they involve intellectual and substantive matters, but animosity is no way to promote commitment and dedication. Likewise, friendship and amiability are desirable, but not at the expense of objectivity and professionalism.

Hold joint seminars on matters of material concern

Discussion of topics other than everyday affairs helps bring out problems and issues and encourages collaboration, fellowship and the learning that allows adaptation to new circumstances.

Formally evaluate the agency's performance

Invite your agency's participation in the process, including its evaluation of you as a client. A productive, mutually beneficial relationship requires constant vigilance.

While this is admittedly a very long list of directives, I truly believe that every one of these steps is critical to building a solid and successful relationship between a client and its agency. If both parties adhere to these guidelines – and nurture a relationship of open communication, strategic agreement and mutual respect – there is a high likelihood that long-term business results will be achieved.

Now we will turn to a discussion of two practical methods for ensuring that an agency and its client are well matched and are working cohesively together. Specifically, we will discuss two formal, foolproof systems our firm developed during the 1970s: 1) The process by which the right communications partner is selected, and 2) The process by which a mutually beneficial compensation agreement is negotiated.

Even when these Guidelines for maximizing a client-agency partnership are followed, marketers sometimes need to identify a new communications partner. There can be many reasons for this. The marketer may want to replace its current agency because: 1) A product conflict has developed, 2) Sales are disappointing and there is a perception that the advertising is to blame, 3) New management is in place and wants to shop the business elsewhere, 4) Management is dissatisfied with the services and product being provided, or 5) The personal relationship between advertiser and agency has deteriorated beyond repair. Compensation is also sometimes the reason, although this issue has largely been addressed by the implementation of the tailored agency compensation agreement, which I will describe later in this Lesson.

Author's Contribution:
The creation of a system for identifying the right communications agency partner

As we've established, there are times when it makes sense for an advertiser to select a new **Commmunications Agency.** At one time, changing agencies was done arbitrarily and without much fanfare. It wasn't unusual for the head of a company to offer his account to a friend or to a popular agency. Fortunately, today the process is much more strategic and systematized. Back in 1974, however, when *Toyota Motors,* for whom we had done a number of consulting assignments, asked our firm to help it select a new agency, the system we created represented a serious departure from accepted practices. The executives at *Toyota* asked our firm to determine a way to have several agencies they were interested in pitch their business. So we developed a systematic method for orchestrating a competition between more than one agency – one we went on to repeat more than 50 times. Frankly I believe the method was so good that most advertisers who used it remained satisfied with the winning agency for a long time. *Toyota* is still with the agency it selected with our help over 40 years ago.

The Competitive Agency Search Process

The value of a systematic **Competitive Agency Search Process** cannot be underestimated. It is the best way an advertiser can separate agency fact from agency fiction. From the agency's standpoint, a new business presentation forces its management to take stock, to articulate what it stands for, to sharpen its focus. No matter how it's done, it exposes an agency's true qualities, especially if it's asked to demonstrate how it can fulfill the advertiser's specific needs.

Equally important, a properly designed **Competitive Agency Search Process** forces the marketer to make its needs explicit, to take careful stock of its situation and to consider the key people involved with the agency's output. Thus, when management finally makes a decision, they will know the true rationale for it and can be assured that their own people will be satisfied with the choice. Moreover, a competitive selection process gives the company the basis for evaluating the agency once it's on board and for holding it accountable over time. Finally, it gives the marketer the basis for judging the compensation arrangement it might wish to make with its agency.

I'll now describe the basic approach our firm developed to assist our clients in selecting a new agency. You'll see that it requires a significant commitment of time and resources by both parties. The system requires careful oversight as it is logistically involved, but it works well. It has helped both large- and small-budget advertisers find agencies that met their needs. In my opinion, it's the only professional way to make a choice if the client's aim is to get the best agency it can.

Picking an agency is much more complex than picking a top-level executive. It's more like picking five executives at once and judging how well they'll perform as a team on the advertiser's behalf. Moreover, the candidates the advertiser deals with are professional "selling organizations" and are good at harnessing their resources for a strong one-shot showing. Thus, a client must be especially vigilant in evaluating agency pitches.

The key to an effective selection process is what I call honest exposure – getting the candidate agencies to reveal themselves, warts and all, on those matters that are material to the client. As in a marriage, you never get a perfect mate. What you strive for is a firm with the fewest negatives on those factors that matter the most, and one with whom you are compatible. Unfortunately, you can't usually discern this from a two-hour dog-and-pony show. It takes much more time and effort for a client to get to know its suitors. It requires putting them through an involved process and, to some extent, placing them under stress. But the more time the client spends with each agency, the more it's apt to learn.

The approach our firm developed for agency searches recognizes the intricacies of making a sound selection. The entire process takes about three months and involves six basic steps. Yes, I said three months. Now you will see why.

Step 1: Formulate the evaluative criteria

This first step in the **Competitive Agency Search Process** is the most critical one because it affects everything else in the process. In it the client formulates the needs it expects the agency to meet if the relationship between the two is to be acceptable. These needs become the criteria by which the advertiser evaluates each agency. They're also extremely important in deciding what the candidate agencies are expected to demonstrate in their various meetings with the advertiser.

These criteria are developed by interviewing the people at the client's company who will interface with the agency in order to determine what they truly need and expect. These needs are then synthesized, committed to writing and reviewed and prioritized with the client. The goal is to create a precise written document of what the client expects and can sign off on. Normally, there are two goals in defining these criteria.

The first goal is to identify objective criteria, such as agency size and location, services offered, conflicts, relationships with other organizations and experience with similar business. These criteria are usually used in an initial screening of candidates to narrow them down to a reasonable number. The second goal is to develop subjective criteria. This will be measured throughout the search, and wlll serve as the basis for the final evaluation of the candidates.

Step 2: Screen the candidates

The second step of the agency search process is the initial screening of candidate agencies. In this step, initial objective screening criteria are applied to all of the agencies in the search. This is also the time to look at some of the agencies' work. Used correctly, the screening criteria can quickly narrow the number of candidates to eight or ten, which keeps the selection process focused. To consider more than this number of agencies is unnecessary if you've done a good job with the screening criteria. Doing this part of the process well saves a lot of time, money, and wear and tear. It also guarantees that you will get an agency you can live with.

Step 3: Design and implement the selection process

The third step of the agency search is to outline the specific process the client should follow in making the selection. It includes but isn't limited to:

- Delineating all the steps included in the remainder of the process
- Describing the logistics involved
- Outlining what material is needed to implement the process
- Preparing agendas and questions to be used in meetings
- Deciding what speculative material, if any, to request from candidate agencies

- Preparing the evaluation forms needed to make a selection

This step, like all the others, must be tailored to the client's specific needs. The number of meetings needed for candidates to show their ability to meet the client's subjective needs and expectations are determined. If, as in most cases, the client wants the candidates to do speculative work, three meetings of varying lengths, each with a separate purpose, will be required.

Step 4: Conduct three formal client-agency meetings

Obviously, the entire search process will require multiple meetings of people at different levels and who perform different functions (account, creative, media, research) at the agency. But here is a description of what should take place at the three formal meetings I described above – between the key decision makers for the client and the leadership of the prospective agency.

Meeting 1: Meeting between client management and agency principals

The first formal meeting involves the major principal in the agency plus one additional executive of the agency's choosing. The purpose is to determine whether the agency is in a position to take the business, whether it wants the business, whether the basic philosophy of the agency's management is compatible with the client's and whether the chemistry at the top is satisfactory. It's amazing what can be learned at such a meeting.

This meeting is a crucial first step because the agency's management plays a major role in every client-agency relationship. Based on this meeting, some of the candidates are likely to fall by the wayside, so it's an effective way to winnow down the candidate list.

Meeting 2: Agency credential meeting

The second formal meeting is intended to assess the agency's credentials. The client is wise to devote a substantial amount of time at each agency, perhaps the better part of a day. The marketer is basically evaluating what the agency has done for its current clients and how that experience relates to the marketer's business and its needs. It's comparable to interviewing several candidates for a key executive position. Before you choose one to work with, you usually have to spend considerable time with him or her. Too much is at stake not to.

Typically, in these meetings, the agency first provides a formal presentation, demonstrating its ability to address the needs outlined in the search criteria document. This should be followed by a tour the agency and a casual meeting with key agency people. The client should use this opportunity to ask questions, and to discuss any position papers submitted by the agency.

This meeting provides a chance to see an agency in some depth – its resources, work, people and facilities. If the client spends enough time with the agency at this stage, it can determine whether it is competent and trustworthy and whether it would be comfortable working with the agency – the most critical overall criteria in picking the right agency.

Meeting 3: Speculative presentation

The final formal meeting is the speculative presentation, where an agency presents an actual end product (an ad campaign, a strategic plan or a media plan) for one of the brands being pitched. Many advertisers don't feel comfortable basing their choice on work the agency has done for others; for them, speculative presentations are a must. I strongly believe in speculative work. It's the best way to learn how an agency works, thinks and operates under pressure – and also how the agency presents material. The speculative meeting actually involves two stages.

The first stage in this process is a preliminary orientation session in which the client (typically, the brand team) explains to the final candidates what speculative work they would like to have prepared. Here the agency is given the background information they'll need to do an effective job. The type of speculative work requested depends on what can best help the advertiser make an intelligent choice. One client might request work that demonstrates how the agency thinks strategically and deals with difficult issues. Another might want to see how the agency buys media and handles its administration. A third might want to see a sample execution of a specific brand's advertising strategy. The client generally pays the agency fees for speculative work. If finished advertising is requested, the cost to the client will be higher. However, if the advertising is good enough, it can actually be used if that agency is chosen, though in my experience, this rarely occurs.

In the second stage of the speculative process, the candidates show their final product to the client. It is critical that all of the client's decision makers are in this meeting because it is their best opportunity to see the agency in the capacity of potential partner as both strategic thinker and conscientious executor.

Step 5: Develop a formal compensation arrangement

The fourth step in an agency search is to design a compensation arrangement that is equitable to both parties and outlines what the client expects to pay for the agency's services. This is something for which my firm also developed a systematic approach, as you will see later in this Lesson. My experience, and that of most advertising people today, suggests that a cost-based fee structure makes the most sense. But every arrangement must be tailored to the client's desires and acceptable to the agency involved. This is best achieved through a careful analysis of the agency's anticipated costs, the structure of the account and its profit expectations. Preferably, the finalists should all agree to the same compensation package before a choice is made. That way, compensation isn't the basis for choosing the agency.

Step 6: Make the final selection

The final step in the search process is deciding which candidate best meets the client's needs and expectations. This step is generally easy if the process has been systematic and dispassionate. Having an objective, disinterested facilitator overseeing the process helps ensure that the final choice is based on the selection criteria, rather than extraneous issues that are bound to enter the picture. During this session, it's best to have evaluation forms to refer to. Only once in all the reviews with which I have been involved did I experience difficulty at this point in the process. The key executives could not agree on the choice, and it became apparent to me that the head of the company wanted to retain the incumbent. His real aim was to get the existing agency to reduce an already low fee arrangement. The search itself was a sham. Regrettably, my partner and I failed to identify this in advance.

In summary, I hope I have convinced you of the value of a carefully articulated, systematic approach to identifying the right communications agency partner. Clearly, this process is by necessity complicated, expensive and somewhat onerous. However, if the right consulting firm effectively executes the search, the end result should satisfactorally address the client's strategic and practical needs and, most importantly, should produce a solid client-agency partnership which will generate excellent business results over the long term.

I can't emphasize enough that, no matter how many times a firm conducts a similar search (and we did it over 50 times), the systematic method must always be tailored to meet the specific needs and desires of the client involved. In closing, I would like to share with you an anecdote which I believe communicates better than my words ever could the importance of judiciously executing every step in the client-agency search process.

Case Study: Toyota Motors

An experience our firm had early in our search days points out how critical every element in the search process is, particularly in personal selling. Let me explain what happened in a preliminary meeting with a major advertising agency that was soliciting the *Toyota Motors* account.

We were in the initial meeting with senior management and were sitting around a coffee table in the elegant oak-paneled office of a prestigious agency. The CEO of the agency offered coffee to my client, *Toyota's* Marketing Director. The CEO poured the coffee from a plastic container into plastic cups with a cigarette brand name imprinted on them. In the process, he spilled some coffee on the table.

At a caucus meeting following the solicitation presentation, I asked for comments from the *Toyota* team. The Marketing Director preempted the discussion by saying we should not bother to go any further because under no circumstances would he offer the agency the *Toyota* business. I asked why. He said it was because the CEO had done such a sloppy job serving him coffee that morning. Not only was he repulsed by the branded plastic cups, but spilling the coffee was enough to disqualify the agency. He was convinced that it showed disrespect for him and his team, and also suggested that the agency must view *Toyota* as a minor player in the industry.

At the time, I thought this was a bit of an over-reaction, but after doing a few more searches, I recognized that the *Toyota* executive was correct in his assessment. In soliciting such a large piece of business, one should not make too many errors, because the winners are often those who make the fewest errors. His view was that a sales presentation is like an opera performance. If the opera diva sang off-key, you'd want your money back. An executive seeking your business should be held to the same standard.

We've now established the systematic selection process which leads to the creation of a successful client-agency relationship. Once this relationship is in place, the next step is to finalize the payment structure, ensuring that it will best meet the needs of both participants and will lead to positive business results in the marketplace. As I mentioned above, a preliminary review of compensation is one of the key steps in the search process. However, as you'll see, creating a mutually beneficial compensation agreement requires its own formal process.

Author's Contribution:
The development of a tailored agency compensation agreement to ensure results

In 1973, I gave a speech in which I declared the traditional 15% commission dead. Needless to say, my pronouncement was met with derision from the agency community and enthusiasm from marketers eager to improve their business's bottom line. In essence, this speech was the beginning of a process which moved the industry away from the standard 15% commission-based model to a labor-based fee structure. While the system was met with skepticism, I believe it resulted in a more efficient and effective means of equitably compensating agencies for their work. Today about 90% of client-agency agreements are labor-based.

How and how much a communications agency is compensated, especially when the stakes are high, is a complex business that requires time, knowledge, experience, negotiating skill, understanding, political acumen, diplomacy, discipline and an established method. This is the perfect situation for outsourcing. A good consultant with these skills can help a client come to equitable terms with an agency so that both parties are satisfied with the terms they've established for working collaboratively – and are turning out an effective product.

The compensation agreements our firm developed were based solely on the specific client's requirements. We tailored them so that agencies got to use a higher-than-industry-average profit on the account while clients got substantial savings over the 15% commission system every year in which the new compensation package was in effect. Because of the fee-schedule feature we devised, which took into account possible future variations in billings, and therefore workload, these compensation arrangements had great longevity. Over the years, our firm negotiated approximately 200 such agreements, creating the standard model for what is practiced across most industries today.

Guidelines for an Equitable Client-Agency Partnership

It goes without saying that a rational and reasonable method for compensating agencies must satisfy the concerns of both advertisers and agencies. Over the course of our work, our firm identified several Guidelines that are essential for achieving an equitable partnership between parties. I want to stress that these Guidelines are not aimed at getting the lowest price for the advertiser. Rather their purpose is to ensure that both parties get the deal that will be best for the business (and their relationship) over the long term. Here then are Guidelines, expressed here from the client's perspective, for ensuring the development of a compensation agreement which is beneficial to both advertisers and their clients.

Agree to a clear plan for negotiations

Establish a negotiating stance which recognizes that both sides must feel satisfied at the end of the process. Negotiation is a cooperative enterprise; common interests must be sought and everyone must feel that they won something.

Ensure the agreement meets both parties' needs

Develop a compensation system which gives the advertiser full value for his money, allowing it to pay only for those services it wants and not for unwanted or unused services. A standard commission doesn't fulfill advertiser's needs. I don't, however, recommend that the advertising functions be disaggregated. On the contrary, there should be no incentive to reduce the agency's role in providing the four intrinsic services – account management, creative, media and research. I'm suggesting instead that differing levels of these services can be adjusted to meet the individual advertiser's needs.

Ensure solid financial results

Make sure that the agency will make a reasonable profit for its efforts without impairing its ability to maintain its professional resources and to create an effective product. Agreeing to the lowest price possible won't satisfy this criterion. An agency must be able to obtain a fair return for its investment of time and money. It must be allowed to make enough profit to reinvest some of its income to expand or improve its own business. Nor is it fair to expect an agency to lose money because of budget cuts that are sudden or beyond its control.

Avoid windfall profits

Eliminate the possibility of an agency's making a windfall profit because of an advertiser's billings – rather than the agency's service or performance. This guideline obviously turns on the meaning of "windfall." Most people would agree that a windfall occurs when an advertiser increases it advertising budget substantially but the agency needs to make little or no additional effort to handle the increased billings. If the agency must accept an upside limit, obviously the advertiser must give the agency downside protection.

Eliminate unnecessary expenses

Provide an incentive to both sides to eliminate unnecessary costs and allow the resultant efficiencies to be mutually shared. Any system that promotes make-work is undesirable. Any system that doesn't control overzealous brand managers from getting the agency to spin its wheels endlessly for little purpose is defective. Any system that allows the agency to do speculative work without the advertiser's knowledge and interest is bound to create dissatisfaction.

Let the agency run its business

Permit the agency to manage its own business affairs without client interference. Advertisers have enough to manage in their own companies. They should seek a compensation system that is easy to administer, doesn't require extensive auditing, rarely needs revision or renegotiation, operates within an environment of mutual trust, and is consistently applicable to all clients yet flexible enough to handle variable circumstances.

A compensation arrangement that which follows these Guidelines fully protects both parties.

The Tailored Compensation Agreement

Our firm developed a formal four-step process for developing an equitable *Tailored Compensation Agreement.* No matter how small the project, we did not neglect to execute any of the four prescribed steps. I believe that so many clients relied on our firm's services over the years because our process showed sensitivity, creativity, practicality and fairness to all. For our purposes, we will assume that the agreement being negotiated is between a client and its existing agency.

Step 1: Assess the client's needs

The first step in negotiating an equitable agreement is to carefully and methodically assess the client's needs. Our firm began by conducting management interviews. We met individually with the executives at the client who were involved in the advertising process – those who either dealt directly with the agency or had an impact on advertising-related decisions. We used these executive interviews for factual input, to stimulate insight and to identify attitudes.

Our goal was to determine which services the client was currently getting from the agency, which ones should be continued, which were unnecessary and which, if any, should be added. This is a critical step, because what the client pays for should be tied to what it wants and gets. We used these executive interviews for factual input and to stimulate insight and reflect attitudes.

Next we developed preliminary criteria. Based on the results of our management interviews, we drafted and submitted to the client a set of criteria for evaluating an equitable agency arrangement. These criteria covered both operational and financial standards, which would serve as the basis for the compensation arrangement.

The third step was an internal data analysis during which we collected and reviewed the client's own financial and operational data relevant to agency compensation. Along with the information gathered from the agency, these data enabled us to estimate the savings the client could realize with a new compensation arrangement.

Step 2: Solicit agency input

We then obtained agency information using a comprehensive questionnaire we asked the agency to fill out. We elicited information about its organization and the staffing it used for a typical account – its costs, revenues, and profits on the client's business for the previous few years, with a projection for the next year – and the amount of media billings the client purchased. Every variable was precisely defined. We also asked the agency to submit a position paper outlining its viewpoint on compensation.

Because we conducted so many negotiations, our firm developed a very reliable method of evaluating and comparing agency financial information and staffing systems. Our fundamental focus was on direct costs related to the four basic agency services: account management, creative, media and research. We conducted an analysis of this evaluative material.

Finally, we analyzed all the data in conjunction with the current agency contract and agreed-upon criteria to determine the arrangement that was needed. We then delivered our report and specific recommendations to the client in both written form and as an oral presentation. If the client supported our recommendation for the new arrangement, we went on to the second phase.

Step 3: Develop a formal compensation agreement

Once we had an agreement in principal from management, our firm then went to work developing a formal compensation arrangement. Key to this process was explicitly articulating the following:

- A variable fee schedule ranging above and below a base billings level, which hinged on the agency's total costs of providing the specified required services, plus an agreed-upon reasonable profit.
- An agency profit-protection feature that guaranteed the agency a minimum profit level on the downside and provided for sharing of excess profits with the client, if profits exceeded a stipulated level on the upside.
- An incentive bonus plan dependent on agency performance.

Finally, we devised the new arrangement to satisfy the established criteria for equitable compensation. An important goal here was to eliminate compensation as an issue in terms of the day-to-day relationship between the client and agency. Nothing can undermine trust and confidence more quickly than a preoccupation with compensation details. We presented our draft recommendation to the client for review and, if necessary, modification.

Step 4: Negotiate the arrangement

This final phase was completed in three parts. First we prepared a pro forma contract incorporating the recommended compensation arrangement and whatever other material matters were needed to protect both parties. Then we met with the agency, presented the new arrangement and explained the rationale behind it. Finally, we helped the client negotiate the agreement with the agency, adjusting it to adress any concerns expressed by either side. We rarely encountered serious problems getting agencies to cooperate throughout this process.

In the end, with occasional minor tweaking, all 200 of the tailored agreements we negotiated were signed by the clients and agencies – and then everybody got to down to work.

Case Study: A Sample Compensation Agreement

Perhaps the best way to demonstrate the efficiency and effectiveness of a ***Tailored Agency Compensation Agreement*** is to provide an example. This example, albeit historical at this point, reflects the critical role played by careful planning, consideration and analysis. While it is technical in nature, I believe that it is an excellent illustration of how a fairly negotiated, mutually beneficial agreement can help foster a solid client-agency relationship.

After assessing the needs of the client – a very large multi-brand manufacturer – we decided that a sliding-scale commission based on billing volume was appropriate. The agreement specified that for each of its brands, the client would pay for basic agency service using a sliding scale of commissions from 20% to 8% on media billing, depending on billing size. The agency's basic service comprised strategic marketing and advertising counsel; development and execution of advertising ideas and campaigns; media analysis, plans, and placement; and billing and paying all media and production supplies. The client also would pay a supplementary fee for all other agency services on each brand.

The agency charged for all research on a cost basis, including all out-of-pocket, time, and overhead charges; production of advertising and all other non-media services in accordance with a schedule of special services; and all work involved in the creation, development and testing of new-market entries before national introduction. We also built in a provision stipulating that if the agency's pretax profit on the total account – meaning all brands combined, whether national, regional, test or developmental – exceeded 2% of actual media billings, the client and agency would share all excess pretax profit. Bear in mind that 2% of billing is the equivalent of 13.3% of 15% commission, which is a pretty good deal for the agency. With a pretax profit in excess of 2% to 3.5%, 60% of the excess went to the client and 40% went to the agency. With an excess exceeding 3.5%, the client kept 80% while the agency kept 20%.

To make the agreement equitable, if the agency's pretax profit on the total account was less than 2% of actual media billings, the client shared the deficit with the agency. For amounts between 1% and 1.9%, the client paid 60% of the deficit while the agency absorbed 40%. For 1% to 0.5%, the client paid 80% of the deficit while the agency absorbed 20%. For less than 0.5%, the client paid 100%. This is good protection for the agency.

All outside services (which were delineated in a written document) were charged at net out-of-pocket cost, including research other than regular syndicated media research, extraordinary telephone charges, and travel, but excluding print. These net costs were added to billings without any commission or fee added. Finally, all costs were reviewed on a semi-annual basis, and, whenever any unusual change in costs was anticipated by either the agency or client, a change was made in the agreement.

This agreement was negotiated in the 1970s, thus there are many ways in which it might be handled differently in today's more complicated and sophisticated marketplace. Nevertheless, I believe it shows how a negotiated fee structure can be equitable to and protective of both sides.

Today marketers who use performance-based compensation agreements report smoother relationships with their agencies – more teamwork, respect and commitment to the work. The system encourages agencies and clients to collaborate more by focusing on common goals.

Conclusion

As we said at the outset of this Lesson, the best opportunity for brands to have success in the marketplace is when they are managed by a client-agency team which has a solid agreement on strategic goals and expectations. Marketers who undertake a rigorous and systematic approach to both selecting their agency and to negotiating its compensation agreement are in the best position to achieve both a copacetic working relationship and successful business results.

We have come at last to the end of our six Lessons. It is my hope that they have provided you with a better appreciation for the critical role which marketing plays in creating business success. I hope I have convinced you of the fundamental value of a strong brand identity – and of the critical role that well-executed, strategic marketing planning, backed by meaningful, scientifically-based consumer research, and supported by solid client-agency partnerships, plays in business success. Further, I hope that you will incorporate these Lessons into the day-to-day operations of whatever business you are in, and that you will experience success both in your personal career and with your business in the marketplace.

Conclusion

"Who steals my purse steals trash...but he that filches from me my good name robs me of that which not enriches him, and makes me poor indeed."

– *William Shakespeare, Othello*

It is my hope that, over the course of these Lessons, I have convinced you that, as was evident in the 16th century, there is nothing more important than a good name. In the centuries to come, communications tools, consumer needs, technology and the marketplace will inevitably change, but one thing will always remain the same: the fundamental value of a strong brand identity.

In my six decades as a practitioner, I have seen time and again how the Lessons outlined in this book are key to the effective management of brands for long-term sustainability. In fact, one could argue that these Lessons are essentially core principles which will likely endure six decades more.

These core principles can be summarized as follows:
- Build and protect a strong brand identity
- Design a consumer-driven, meaningful brand strategy
- Undertake a disciplined strategic marketing planning process
- Conduct systematic, quantitatively-based market research
- Ensure effective, well-targeted marketing communications
- Build productive, mutually beneficial agency-client relationships

The Challenges for Marketing

The effective implementation of these core principles by a determined and resourceful marketer should lead directly to success in the marketplace. To achieve this success in the future, however, marketers must be aware of and prepared to respond to several important and increasingly challenging marketplace conditions.

Let's take a closer look at these challenges – and learn how fundamental marketing tools can help vanquish them.

The globalization of business

In the future, the globalization of business will continue and the production and marketing playing fields will flatten, so that more and more countries outside the developed Western world will be important players in economic activity. The ongoing threat of global financial instability will affect the way companies make strategic and investment decisions. In addition, the easy flow of information and flexibility offered by increasingly sophisticated technology will further increase global competition and tighten new market opportunities. It will be more critical than ever for business leaders to use their best competitive weapon, marketing, to retain brand leadership and to ensure a company's long-term financial health.

The expansion of new technology

There can be no doubt that the expansion of new forms of technology will improve the rate at which business can be developed, practiced and evaluated. Developments in the pipeline offer interesting opportunities. Biotechnology, miniaturization and nanotechnology all show explosive potential for the creation of innovative new products and services, which is essential for economic growth. Energy conservation will play a major role in the next decade, as will the novel methods by which products will be manufactured and distributed. Smart marketers must be on the lookout for – and prepared to quickly adapt to – evolving technological advancements.

Management focus on short-term profits

Regrettably, there continues to be substantial interest by top management in generating accelerated short-term profits in lieu of implementing cost controls and improving internal efficiencies. Rather than demanding short-term profit results, smart management will focus on innovative marketing functions. These include: 1) Expanding into new geographical areas, 2) Going after carefully vetted new markets, 3) Increasing the incidence and frequency of use in existing product and service categories, and

4) Investing in marketing communications. Taking advantage of these opportunities will put brands in a much better position to achieve sustainable, incremental profitable growth.

The polarization of retail distribution

What we have been witnessing over the past two decades is the dramatic unraveling of the prevalent and powerful pull-marketing formula that permitted many businesses to be successful. As technology becomes more omnipresent, competition between the internet and brick-and-mortar stores will continue to heat up. Shrewd marketers will have to find ways to satisfy both purchase points – and to take advantage of the unique properties of each. Continuously evaluating a product line, judiciously implementing online and in-store promotional activity, as well as creatively using communications tools to reach consumers in a multitude of venues, will be key to this process.

Failure to keep marketing at the forefront of strategic planning

Finally, as competition becomes more global, consumers become more wary and profit demands increase, the need for strategically-based brand franchise-building will be even more critical. Thus, the nurturing of brands must be paramount. This effort has multiple components, including: 1) Building powerful and defensible brand identities with protected trademarks, 2) Designing market research which harnesses emerging technologies and brings insight and relevant understanding to the planning process, and 3) Reducing the reliance on price as the marketing tool of choice and re-establishing the power of advertising and its collateral marketing services. Finally, at its very core, marketing success will continue to be dependent on disciplined strategic thinking and flawless execution.

The Customer is King

It is my sincere hope that my Lessons have clarified the tools which are at your disposal in your quest to deliver strong business results in an increasingly globally-connected and technologically-dominated world. Now is the time for business leaders of tomorrow like you to dramatically improve the use of marketing effectiveness – and to help the rest of the world do the same.

Retailer John Wanamaker, one of the early developers of the department store in the United States, is famously known for his axiom: "The customer is king." By this he meant that it was the role of the seller is to satisfy the buyer, that nothing is more important. In other words, it all comes down to one transaction: between the buyer and the seller – or, for our purposes, between the marketer and the consumer. At its most fundamental level, therefore, the future success of business depends on managers like you conscientiously identifying what the customer wants – and effectively using strategic marketing tools to deliver it best.

Acknowledgements

One of the most important Lessons I learned in writing this book was that it would have been impossible without the assistance of some very talented, dedicated and generous people.

Four individuals played a critical role in the editing and production of the book: Kenny Bartlett, Dick Elfenbein, Jackson Hartell and Marjorie Miller.

For sharing my passion for marketing and for joining me in my quest to improve business practices, I am indebted to my brilliant colleagues and business partners: Joel Baumwoll, Pete Bogda, Stan Canter, Jim Heekin, Dick Lessler and Carl Spielvogel.

My children, Jon Achenbaum, Lisa Kounitz and Martha Bratt, all provided encouragement and the occasional constructive criticism.

My daughter-in-law, Barb Achenbaum, was extremely helpful in editing and overseeing the final preparations of this manuscript.

I would also like to extend my gratitiude to Jacqueline Reid Wachholz and to the John W. Hartman Center at Duke University for their extensive efforts cataloging the output of my six decades of work, and for giving it such a prestigious permanent home.

And finally, I dedicate this book to the important women in my life: Barbara, Lee and Shirley. Each in her own special way encouraged me to be a better marketer and made me a better person.

About the Author

A marketing veteran of the "Mad Men" era, Alvin Achenbaum was responsible for many of the tectonic changes which helped shape today's advertising and marketing worlds. Named one of *Advertising Age's* most influential advertising executives of the 20th century, Achenbaum was instrumental in establishing many of today's common industry practices.

Over a remarkable 60-year career, Achenbaum advised leading global marketers, including *Procter & Gamble, GE, Toyota* and *Nestlé*, on how to use marketing tools to improve the economic value of their businesses. He held senior executive positions at four major advertising agencies in New York City: *McCann-Erickson, J. Walter Thompson, Grey Advertising*, where he created the market research department, and *Backer, Spielvogel, Bates Worldwide*, where he served as vice chairman, overseeing all professional services. For 40 years, Achenbaum was chairman of a series of preeminent marketing consulting firms which provided companies with systematic tools for addressing complex business challenges.

Always a champion of the critical role marketing plays in economic success, Achenbaum introduced many of the business leaders of the last half century to such fundamental concepts as: 1) Building brand equity, 2) Undertaking disciplined strategic marketing planning, 3) Using systematic quantitative research as a guide, and 4) Maximizing agency-client relationships.

Achenbaum holds a Bachelor's degree in Business Economics from UCLA and a Master's degree in Business Economics from Columbia University.

For more information, please visit www.achenbauminstitute.com